Outstanding Studies in

Early American History

EDITED BY
John Murrin
Princeton University

A Garland Series

The Puritan Apocalypse

New England Eschatology in
the Seventeenth Century

Joy Gilsdorf

Garland Publishing, Inc.
NEW YORK & LONDON 1989

Library of Congress Cataloging-in-Publication Data

Gilsdorf, Joy.
    The Puritan apocalypse : New England eschatology in the
seventeenth century / Joy Gilsdorf.
   p. cm. — (Outstanding studies in early American history)
Thesis (Ph.D.)—Yale, 1964.
     Bibliography: p.
     ISBN 0–8240–6181–0 (alk. paper)
     1. Puritans—New England—History—17th century.
     2. Eschatology—
History of doctrines—17th century. 3. New England—Church
history—17th century. I. Title. II. Series.
BX9355.N35G55 1989
236'.08'825—dc20   89–7763

Printed on acid-free, 250-year-life paper

MANUFACTURED IN THE UNITED STATES OF AMERICA

TABLE OF CONTENTS

PREFACE

Modern historians by and large have been loath to attribute apocalyptic aspirations to the Puritans who settled in America. Their reluctance in part derives from their conclusion that the social conservatism of these Puritans precluded the kind of apocalyptic fanaticism associated with, say, the Fifth Monarchy men. (So far as it goes, this conclusion is quite correct. The New England Puritans did not wish to reconstruct radically the institutions of the society which had produced them, although they did want to change its moral tone.) Another reason for their reluctance is that it has always been easy to dismiss the apocalyptic speculations of an earlier age. Men who attempt to predict the immediate future--whether by correlating contemporary events with biblical prophecies or by any other means--invariably make themselves liable to the disdain of later, "wiser" generations. For the Puritans such correlations not infrequently provided the occasion for sustained and vitriolic polemics against the Catholics. These passages show the Puritans at their worst and no doubt have contributed to the feeling that the Apocalyptic commentaries in which they are imbedded should not be taken seriously. Nevertheless, as I hope to show, the apocalyptic ideas of the New England Puritans were central to their Weltanschauung, materially affecting such diverse things as their conception of church polity and their philosophy of history.

A word about my use of the term Puritan is in order here. So far as the colonists in America are concerned, I have confined it to the inhabitants of Massachusetts, Connecticut, New Haven, and Plymouth. These colonies share similar--though not identical--views on church polity. Rhode Island, as everyone knows, represented a considerable departure from the "New England Way." As this last statement suggests, the basis for my definition of Puritans in England is a comparatively narrow one. In order to relate eschatological ideas to other contemporary concerns, it has been convenient to define Puritans as those who linked their demands for reformation to changes in church polity. It may well be that to distinguish them in this manner is to miss the whole point of their demand for greater purity. Nevertheless, I believe this definition is meaningful when related to their eschatology.

I would like to express my appreciation for the criticism and advice of Prof. Sydney E. Ahlstrom and for the tolerant and helpful guidance of Prof. Edmund S. Morgan. Naturally, the responsibility for any errors of fact or opinion is my own. Finally, I wish to thank my husband for his unfailing support. Without it, this dissertation would not have been completed.

Chapter I.

THE KINGDOM IN HISTORY

Judgment Day, as the Puritans were fond of pointing out, was the moment when the three great works of God--creation, new creation or redemption, and providence--would be consummated in a final, all-encompassing revelation of God's might and majesty. "The Works of Creation and the Mystery of Redemption, and the strange Mysteries of Providence, and Wisdom, and Righteousness of God in all, will then be revealed to the Admiration of men and Angels for ever."[1] That the works of God in the world and history were mysterious, every Puritan would have been quick to admit. At the most mundane level, it was difficult to explain why success frequently came to worldly men while calamity overtook the godly. Yet if the world as it was was inexplicable, the world to come was not; and the expectation that he would one day comprehend these three great works was the saint's ever-present sustenance. In the midst of mystery and uncertainty he knew that God had created the world and placed man within it for a purpose--a purpose which no Puritan ever doubted was His own glory. But what worked to God's glory worked also to man's good, and it was upon this confidence that Puritans were prepared to yield themselves up to God's will. It was this very willingness to entrust his destiny to divine decree that marked out the "predestined" saint. Only those who were capable of such faith in the final, eschatological triumph of good over evil could with some certainty be counted among the number of the elect.

For many of the Puritans who came to America this ability to rest their hopes upon the final outcome of history was fortified by their conviction that the ultimate triumph of good was not far off. Like virtually all Reformation Protestants, they believed that the end of the world was rushing upon mankind and that only a little time stood between the human race and judgment--although few of them would have undertaken to pinpoint the exact date.

---

[1]Increase Mather, The Greatest Sinners Exhorted and Encouraged to Come to Christ (Boston, 1686), 71.

In contrast to medieval theologians who postponed indefinitely
the occurrence of last things and thus stressed the permanence
and unchangeableness of the church, men of the Reformation era
felt themselves to be living in an age in which the church would
be purified and all history brought to the edge of consummation
through the preaching of God's Word.[2]

This belief was in part the outgrowth of the sectarian,
chiliastic heresies that had swept through Europe in the late
Middle Ages. Intent upon undermining papal claims to supremacy,
the sectaries had seized upon the subversive idea of Christ's
imminent return and had identified the Pope as the Antichrist
who must be overthrown before the second coming. Such an
identification served to reinforce their attacks upon the
immorality of the Roman church. When it was combined with a
conception of the true church as a body of the elect,
distinguished from the world by their righteousness, this
repudiation of the Pope became a particularly corrosive element
in the disintegration of medieval Christendom.[3]

Luther himself appropriated these two ideas of
pre-destination and eschatology from the sectaries and
eventually came to believe that the end of the world was not
more than a century away.[4] Profoundly shocked by his
realization that the Roman church would not reform of its own
accord, he had found it easy to identify not only the Pope but

---

[2]T. F. Torrance, Kingdom and Church: A Study in the
Theology of the Reformation (Fair Lawn, N.J., 1956), 3-4.

[3]Roland H. Bainton, The Reformation of the Sixteenth
Century (Boston, 1952), 19.

[4]It should be pointed out, however, that Luther did not
believe the Apocalypse was part of the canon, and that he was
far from dogmatic when it came to apocalyptic speculations.

the institution of the papacy itself with Antichrist. Like the
medieval sectaries, he believed that Christ would shortly return
to confound His antithesis, and he enjoined Christians to look
forward with joy to that time when the salvation of the elect
would finally be completed. But Luther's "discovery" that the
papacy and Antichrist were identical had ramifications that went
far beyond his expectation of Christ's imminent return. Most
important, it led him to the conclusion that the church on earth
could never be disengaged from its secular and hence sinful
involvement with this world. Within the institutional church
two kingdoms--that of the world and that of Christ--existed in a
constant dialectical tension that would not be resolved short of
Judgment Day. The visible church could never be identified with
the Kingdom of Christ as it had been by the Popes. On earth the
Kingdom existed only in the Word of God. Insofar as the Word
was preached and believed, Christ ruled in the hearts of the
elect, who made up a hidden community of believers within the
greater body of the visible church. Until Judgment Day this
reign would always be an invisible one--a secret agency which in
Creation's old age stirred the world into unprecedented turmoil,
but which could be identified with no earthly church or
kingdom. For this reason, in spite of his own apocalyptical
tendencies, Luther repudiated all fanatic attempts to anticipate
Christ's advent and establish the heavenly Kingdom by force. If
the elect could never be identified on earth, no church could
claim absolute purity; nor could the saints band together to
rule the world. To confuse the two kingdoms or to attempt to
shake them out of their dialectical tension was to identify
oneself with Antichrist. As T. F. Torrance has put it, "[the]
apocalyptic for Luther pointed not so much to the engagement of
the Kingdom of God with history, as to its abrupt
termination."[5]

Calvin, on the other hand, rejected the expectation of an
early return of the Lord that had sustained Luther. Instead, he
projected the final cataclysm into an indefinite future and
enjoined the saint to find his encouragement in a daily
witnessing to his faith. "It is far from the Lord to appoint a

---

[5]Torrance, 19.

fixed day as though the Last Judgment were necessarily imminent
. . . He wills rather to educate His disciples in patient
waiting: they must take heart and realize that still many a long
stretch must be traversed before the day of complete
salvation."[6]   But even though Calvin minimized the apocalyptic
element in eschatology, he nevertheless set forth a
fundamentally eschatological view of the church and history that
was to play a great part in Reformed and Puritan thought. For
Calvin was prepared to involved the Kingdom of Christ in history
in a way in which Luther was not. Taking the twin concepts of
predestination and eschatology as the beginning and the end of
salvation, Calvin conceived of the interim between them as a
gradual progress in the direction of perfection. The faith of
individual believers was primarily one of hope. Based on the
security of eternal election, it nevertheless thrived on
constant anticipation of a future fulfillment. In death the
believer achieved a partial fulfillment by entering into the
bliss of heavenly meditation, which he would enjoy until
absolute glory came with Judgment Day. Faith, in fact, was a
kind of transition from eternal predestination to future glory.
The life of the saint on earth was a pilgrim's progress between
calling and consummation--a life of travail in which faith was
sustained by the hope of a heavenly future.

Calvin's emphasis upon progress in faith comes out even more
clearly in relation to the church. Standing as Christ's Kingdom
between His ascension (its beginning) and His second advent (its
end), the church existed in history as the medium in which these
two moments were temporally and eschatologically related. In
one sense the church as the body of the elect had been complete
from eternity. Within history it grew from infancy in the
Israelite nation to maturity in the preaching of Christ, and
with His resurrection it entered into its last age. Thus the
Christian era, according to Calvin, had always contained both
the seeds of growth and the seeds of decay:

---

[6]John Calvin, quoted in Heinrich Quistorp, Calvin's
Doctrine of the Last Things, trans. Harold Knight (London,
1955), 27.

To make the matter clearer, let us suppose two worlds, the
first the old, corrupted by Adam's sin, the other, later in
time, as renewed by Christ. The state of the first creation
has become wholly decayed, and with man has fallen as far as
man himself is concerned. Until, then, a new restitution
can be made by Christ, this Psalm (8) will not be
fulfilled. It hence now appears that here the renovated
world is not that which we hope for after the resurrection
but that which began at the beginning of Christ's Kingdom,
but it will no doubt have its full accomplishment in our
final redemption.[7]

These two worlds, we should note, did not exist in a
fundamentally static tension such as Luther had envisaged but
rather conflicted with one another in a dynamic, progressive
relationship.

The point at which the two worlds most clearly made contact
was the church and more particularly, the visible church. Here
Calvin had to confront a problem common to all the Reformers,
namely, the nature of the relationship of the church to Christ's
Kingdom. In this, its last age, to what extent did the church
participate in the coming glory? Or, to put it another way, how
much of the visible church derived from the corrupt world and
how much from the renewed world? With this problem was involved
a second and perhaps even more crucial one--was it required of
men that they distinguish between the two?

In contrast to Luther who thought of the visible church as
participating in the Kingdom only insofar as it contained a
hidden community of believers, Calvin believed that the Kingdom
existed in the actual, historical communication of the Gospel
or, in other words, that it could be correlated with the
building up of the church by human agency. This was true for
him simply because there was no other way of entering into the
life of salvation than through the church. Indeed the church
was the mother of the saints, conceiving and bearing them,
nourishing and maintaining them until the moment of death.

---

[7]Quoted in Torrance, 121.

"There is no other bond by which the saints can be kept together than by uniting with one consent to observe the order which God has appointed in his Church for learning and making progress."[8]

Given then the fact that for Calvin the Kingdom and the Church were virtually correlative, there still remained the problem of the way in which the order of the church should reflect the perfection (or coming perfection) of the Kingdom; and this brings us back to our second question--did God intend men to judge what was of the Kingdom and what was not in the order of the church? Calvin's answer was that within history the face of the church was and always had been ambiguous. The glory of the Kingdom was nowhere clearly transcribed in the earthly institution. While there must be a fixed form or legitimate polity of church order, such ordinances were neither necessary to salvation nor rigid and inflexible:

[Christ] has not been pleased to prescribe every particular that we ought to observe (he foresaw that this depended on the nature of the times, and that one form would not suit all ages), in them we must have recourse to general rules which he has given, employing them to test whatever the necessity of the Church may require to be enjoined for order and decency. Lastly, as he has not delivered any express command, because things of this nature are not necessary to salvation, and, for the edification of the Church, should be accommodated to the varying circumstances of each age and nation, it will be proper, as the interest of the Church may require, to change and abrogate the old, as well as to introduce new forms.[9]

---

[8]Calvin, Institutes of the Christian Religion, trans. Henry Beveridge (Grand Rapids, Mich., 1953), II, 286.

[9]Ibid., II, 436.

It was always within the power of men to corrupt any
ordinance of God and render it unprofitable. "Men mount the
throne of judgment and, as if they were gods, anticipate the day
of Christ, who alone is appointed by the Father as Judge, allot
to every one his station of honour, assign to some a high place,
and degrade others to the lowest seats."[10] The only proper
way to avoid such arrogance was to measure the church constantly
against the judgment of Christ as revealed in God's Word,
remembering that in this world it must exist as a suffering
servant in the midst of tribulation. Since the Church's true
form would appear only at the end of time, its present forms
should never be regarded as final or as ends in themselves but
rather as interim means for bringing the church ever closer to
its ultimate perfection. The church could not be framed so that
there remained nothing to be amended. Nor could "so great a
building" be finished in a single day. Some further detail
would always require more attention. As humbly as any pilgrim,
therefore, the church should make its way throughout the course
of history, always conscious that the seeds of perfection which
it carried within itself had not yet come to full term. Calvin
described it this way: "The Kingdom of Christ is on such a
footing, that it is every day growing and making improvement,
while at the same time perfection is not attained, nor will be
until the final day of reckoning. Thus both things hold
true--that all things are now subject to Christ, and that thus
subjection will, nevertheless, not be complete until the day of
resurrection, because that which is now only begun will then be
completed."[11]

One of the most important results of Calvin's conception of
the Kingdom as a growing and improving entity was to focus men's
attention upon history as the medium within which it developed.
This in turn tended to dissuade them from attempts to anticipate
the certain maturity of this divine growth. Confident of
salvation, saints were expected to leave the future to God and
concentrate on fulfilling their providentially assigned roles in
the present development of history. By so doing they
contributed to the gradual maturation of the Kingdom--but only

---

[10]Calvin, quoted in Torrance, 135-36.

[11]Quoted in Torrance, 152-153.

as willing servants perform assigned tasks in their Master's
absence. Futhermore in Calvin's theology saints were even
discouraged from speculations about the probable time of their
Master's return. Believers did not desire to
know more about the time of the end than God had set forth in
His Word. The hour of Christ's coming had been deliberately
concealed from men so that they might always be upon the watch
for it. Calvin's conception of the Kingdom, in short, simply
was not conducive to millennial interpretation. Nor is this
surprising since millennialists ordinarily do not expect the
church to achieve earthly perfection through gradual historical
development. For them the millennial reign is <u>not</u> an ideal
condition of the world brought about by the operation of divine
leaven in history--a process prior to and independent of
Christ's second coming. Rather it is a supernatural,
extra-historical irruption of the other world into this one, and
it meets fierce resistance.[12] The normal sphere of action for
Calvinists in all ages naturally came to be the improvement of
the existing world rather than the creation of a totally new
order.

Though Calvin himself abjured any attempt to force the pace
of the Kingdom's growth or even to divine forbidden knowledge
concerning its duration on earth, many men who adhered to one or
another version of Reformed theology did not show such
circumspection. Among these were the Puritans. Like Calvin

---

[12]Strictly speaking, the word "millennialist" here refers
to one who is a pre-millennialist, i.e., one who believes that
the millennium will be inaugurated by the personal appearance of
Christ to judge the world. This belief is often associated with
fanatic action "anticipating" Christ's appearance. The opposite
of this belief is post-millennialism, i.e., the belief that the
millennium will gradually develop within history and that Christ
will appear only after the thousand years has ended. As we
shall see, the lines between these two conceptions of the
millennium are not always sharply drawn. Calvin, of course, is
best described as a-millennial, since the millennium as such had
no place in his theology.

the Puritans were generally not prepared to underwrite their attempts to reform the world with an expectation of Christ's immediate return, but in the late sixteenth and early seventeenth centuries they found great encouragement in the thought that they lived and labored in what was indisputably the world's last age. The historical struggle between good and evil had entered its ultimate phases--howsoever long these might be.

The explanation of this anomaly is simple enough. Like the medieval sectaries, like Luther, Zwingli, Peter Martyr, and indeed like Calvin himself, the Puritans believed that the Pope was Antichrist. Since Antichrist represents Satan's last and most violent attempt to corrupt the entire world before he is finally crushed, his appearance meant that Armageddon must be relatively near. It was obvious to Puritans and their fellow Englishmen that the confrontation between Protestantism and anti-christian Rome was already rapidly separating the world into diametrically opposed camps. Men heard the sermons of the Reformation--the last great preaching of grace--and then chose (as God willed) between good and evil. This division of humanity into saints or sinners could only eventuate in apocalyptic struggle. The only question that remained was how long it would take for the lines to be drawn.

The answers varied but all of them were based upon the interpretation of biblical prophecies--particularly those of the Apocalypse. Naturally the controversy among scholars and theologians was long and hot. Calvin had studiously avoided writing an interpretation of St. John's Revelation, but his followers showed no such restraint. Solving its riddles by diligent research into history became a serious occupation for many Puritans in both Old and New England. All of these men took it for granted that the proper way to interpret the Apocalypse was to correlate its prophecies with historical events, for they all believed that the entire course of history from beginning to end was accurately predicted in this cryptic book. As Thomas Goodwin put it, "the Book of the Revelation is a tragi-comical vision of the occurrences of the world through all times and ages; whereof this may truly be the title,

'The story of Christ's kingdom.'"[13] The story, moreover, told not of vague trends or broad movements but described specific events--the fall of Jerusalem, the conversion of the Jews, Armageddon, and the return of Christ. The interpreter had only to decide which prophecy should be correlated with which historical occurrence in order to arrive at some approximate knowledge of the present progress of the Kingdom. Given their deep conviction that the Pope was Antichrist in conjunction with the outline of history which the Apocalypse spread so intriguingly before them, it is no wonder that godly and sober-minded Puritans often succumbed to the temptation of trying to determine how close history was to "its" goal.

In this occupation they were frequently joined by their compatriots. Englishmen who were not Puritans also believed that the Pope was Antichrist, that prophecy and history were complementary parts of one great continuum, and most of them were equally quick to repudiate any suggestion of millennial fanaticism. Before Puritanism as such even came into being, English reformers were busy educating their countrymen in the history of Christ's Kingdom on earth by using these very ideas--ideas which were, after all, common to most Protestants during the Reformation. These early reformers were particularly concerned with building up the conception of a national Protestant church which would command the devotion and loyalty of all citizens. To this end they wrote a number of works designed to show that sixteenth-century England occupied a vital place in the historical economy of the Kingdom. One of the earliest of these, The Image of Both Churches, was written by John Bale--an English monk who had been converted to the Protestant cause in the reign of Henry VIII, and who subsequently became one of the most ardent and virulent propagandists for the new faith. First published in 1550 after Bale's return from exile on the Continent, The Image of Both

---

[13]The Works of Thomas Goodwin, ed. John C. Miller ("Nichol's Series of Standard Divines: Puritan Period"; Edinburgh, 1863), III, 207.

<u>Churches</u> is an exegesis of the Apocalypse intended to help men distinguish the true church from the false. According to Bale, St. John's vision prophesied the whole course of the church's history from the earliest times to the end of the world, describing in every age not only the "true christian church" but also the "sinful synagogue of Satan." With the aid of Revelation, therefore, men could discern "what the innocent christian church is, with all her justifications and blessings, to the singular comfort of the Lord's true elect; and what the proud synagogue of antichrist is, with her filthy superstitions and plagues."[14] Nor was it difficult to distinguish between the two churches since "the one is maintained by the only preaching of God's pure word, the other by all kinds of Jewish ceremonies and heathenish superstitions."[15]

But even though the true church was maintained by the preaching of God's Word, Bale did not believe that it could be identified with any visible, corporate institution. The true church consisted only of the elect and, since this was so, it had by definition to remain unknown until the end of the world. Nonetheless, Christ's church did have a real existence in history as the continuing struggle between godliness and unrighteousness showed. For Bale the story of the church in all times could be reduced to the ever-recurring struggle between the elect and their innumerable enemies. Satan had begun his attacks against God's chosen almost as soon as the Word was first preached in the persecutions of the Roman emperors. More subtly in the dark clouds of ignorance which soon thereafter moved over the world, the Devil had sought to turn the saints from their faith. Nor was the lot of the elect bettered when Constantine became a Christian, for then there appeared "heretics and unpure ministers, ambitious prelates and false teachers" to plague the true church. These had persisted to the present day.

---

[14]Select Works of John Bale, ed. Henry Christmas ("The Parker Society Publications," I; Cambridge, 1849), 640.

[15]Ibid.

Evident it is . . . what the estate of the christian church was, and is now in these latter days. Such horrible confusion have the antichrists made with their wicked laws and decrees, and with their deceitful doctrine of errors and lies, to uphold their filthy kingdom of pride, sloth, hypocrisy, and beastliness, that scarcely is any thing clean, pure, and godly. ... And thus is it like still to continue to the end of the world.[16]

Nevertheless, Satan and his antichristian minions had not had things entirely their way during the history of the church. One of St. John's prophesies predicts the establishment of a thousand-year reign of Christ on earth during which Satan will be held in bondage.[17] Bale, who was here following St. Augustine, believed that this reign had begun immediately after the Resurrection. Needless to say, Christ's rule had not been a visible government but an invisible dominion in the hearts of the elect. "This revelation respecteth in this point the inward kingdom of Christ, or the hidden congregation of the faithful, whom the world beholdeth with froward eyes. . . . None otherwise were they for all those thousand years vexed of Satan and his cursed members, but as was patient Job, in their outward substance and bodies. No power had he upon their souls all that long season."[18] At the end of the millennium--again as forecast in Revelation--Satan had broken out of his bondage.[19] "Afore that Satan was thus at liberty, he remained

---

[16]Ibid., 322-23.

[17]Rev. 20: 4, 5. "I saw the souls of them that were beheaded for the witness of Jesus, and for the word of God, and which had not worshipped the beast, neither his image, neither had received his mark upon their foreheads, or in their hands; and they lived and reigned with Christ a thousand years. But the rest of the dead lived not again until the thousand years were finished. This is the first resurrection."

[18]Bale, 561.

[19]Rev. 20: 7, 8. "And when the thousand years are expired, Satan shall be loosed out of his prison, and shall go out to deceive the nations which are in the four quarters of the earth, Gog and Magog, to gather them together to battle."

secret in the hearts of evil men. Now is he abroad in their
outward ceremonies and rites, ready to be seen of all
the world, if pride, pomp, haughtiness, and vain-glory may shew
him, or if hypocrisy, error, superstition and all other
devilishness can tell where he is."[20] But even as the Devil
had appeared openly in flagrant sin and corruption (c.1100), he
had been opposed by those over whom he would never have
power--men such as the Waldensians, Wyclif, Huss, Petrarch, and
in Bale's own day, Luther, Melancthon, Bullinger, and Bucer.
The final phase in the war between the people of God and
Antichrist had been initiated and would continue without ceasing
until the Day of Judgment.

This then was the great story of the church which Bale found
set forth in the Apocalypse. Throughout history--though perhaps
less so in the days of the apostles--the elect had had to
struggle with "one general antichrist . . . which hath reigned
in the [visible] church in a manner since the ascension of
Christ."[21] Yet for a thousand years the hidden congregation
of the faithful had had peace. "For though they had in the
world on every side tribulation, yet had they their consciences
quieted in Christ."[22] Now that the Devil had been released
from bondage and raged visibly in the world, the elect were
called to resist him--not by force but by living the life of
godliness. Throughout all their sufferings and tribulations at
the hands of the Devil, God's people could rest secure in their
knowledge of Christ's inevitable return, whether at the end of
the world or at "the particular end of any man." Hence the
faithful, "being here in adversity," could be glad in the
thought that "their deliverance is at hand, and their crown of
immortality not far off."[23] In this manner Bale like Calvin
emphasized the role of hope in the faith of the saints.
Invisible to the eyes of the profane, Christ's church was most
powerful when it seemed to be weakest. "Then reigneth the godly

---

[20]Bale, 562.

[21]Ibid., 442.

[22]Ibid., 564.

[23]Ibid., 625.

number most of all, when they seem to the wicked least of all to
reign, as when they suffer persecution and death for Christ.
For after none other sort reigneth his church here than he
reigned afore them, whose triumph was greatest upon the
cross."[24] According to Bale, tribulation was not only the
most likely lot for the saint, it was essential to his
salvation.

> Nevertheless to the Christian is persecution necessary. For
> here in this life is the patience of the saints proved, and
> their faith required. . . . Only is it faith that all the
> evils of this world by patience overcometh, and so obtaineth
> the victory. The fruit which riseth to eternal life is
> peaceable sufferance in faith. And that must be here in
> this life, where as we are unperfect, to make us
> perfect.[25]

But even though Bale considered the progress of the saint
through the tribulations of this world necessary for the full
realization of faith, he did not like Calvin have any conception
of the growth of Christ's Kingdom in history. Instead Bale's
emphasis throughout his work is on the sameness of the Kingdom
from the first century to the sixteenth. Although he correlated
particular prophesies with historical events, Bale took great
pains to insist that St. John's visions were fulfilled to a
greater or lesser degree in all ages. The hidden congregation
of the faithful, the eternal reign of Christ in the hearts of
His elect, the sufferings of the saints witnessing to the truth
of God's Word--these were constants in the history of the world
and would continue unchanged to its end.

---

[24]Ibid., 567.

[25]Ibid., 436.

If Bale was convinced that the fundamental substance of history--St. Augustine's tension between civitas dei and civitas terrena-- would not alter before Christ appeared to complete the redemption of the elect, he did share the optimistic hope of his fellow reformers that the end was not far off. "Never were more earnest witnesses than are now, and more are like hereafter to follow, till the man of sin be fully known, and his kingdom clearly overthrown."[26] If ever there was a time to bear witness against Antichrist, it was now; and one of Bale's primary purposes was to see that England produced its full share of such men. Bale hoped to convince the entire English people that their participation as a nation in the struggle between the godly and the unrighteous was essential to both their individual and corporate salvation. As one of the first nations to repudiate the antichristian tyranny of the Pope, England clearly had an obligation to lead the rest of the world in witnessing to the truth. Only by freeing the ministry of God's Word from antichristian corruptions and allowing it the full measure of its impact upon the "predestinate elect" could England unequivocally place itself on the side of godliness.

England, however, was not in a position to heed Bale's plea for resistance to Antichrist. Only three years after The Image of Both Churches was published, Queen Mary came to the throne; and Bale was once more forced to flee to the Continent. His work had not been wasted. His apocalyptical scheme of history was picked up by another Marian exile, John Foxe, who used it to provide a framework for his famous Book of Martyrs. When the exiles returned triumphantly to initiate the Elizabethan age, Foxe's story of the English martyrs (first published in 1573) rapidly acquired an influence in the minds of Englishmen second only to that of the Bible. What Foxe did was to fill in Bale's great scheme with "documentary" accounts of the witness of English martyrs through the ages. From virtually apostolic times, according to Foxe, the communion of the elect had existed in England and its members had protested--however uselessly-- against the corruptions of Antichrist. This protest had naturally reached its climax in the persecutions of Queen Mary. Now that God had rescued His people from antichristian oppressions through the agency of Elizabeth, it was up to the

---

[26]Ibid., 391.

English nation to vindicate the sufferings of their martyrs by leading the rest of mankind out of Roman tyranny. It was obvious to Foxe that England under the guidance of its Protestant Queen had been providentially selected to play an essential role in the final downfall of Antichrist.[27]

The lessons which Foxe read in his country's history were soon accepted without question by his compatriots. Part of the reason for this was that by the time the Book of Martyrs was published, the ground had been well prepared by other exiles who had been given important positions in the church upon their return to England. Ever since the accession of Elizabeth men like Archbishop Parker and John Jewel had been extending the idea of the elect to include the conception of England as an elect nation singled out by God to fulfill a special purpose in history.[28] Foxe, by rewriting the history of the church from the viewpoint of an English Protestant, provided the "documentary" historical proof that the English people had been providentially designated for a particular divine purpose. Following the story of English martyrs from Roman times to the reign of Mary, Foxe's readers could hardly escape the conclusion that England had indeed played an important part in the history of the church. Nor, by the end of his book, could they deny that England had a special, apocalyptic mission to carry out in the near future.

In the years during which John Foxe and his fellow reformers were popularizing the apocalyptic image of an elect nation, interest in the interpretation of Relevation itself was growing. Several of the English exiles in Mary's reign had stayed in Zurich, and it is likely that while they were there, they had heard Heinrich Bullinger preach a series of one hundred sermons on the Apocalypse in 1556.

---

[27]A superb exposition of Foxe's ideas and the role which his book played in Elizabethan England is William Haller, The Elect Nation: The Meaning and Relevance of Foxe's Book of Martyrs (New York, 1964).

[28]Ibid., 105.

Bullinger's sermons may even have been a greater influence on their apocalyptic thinking than Bale's work.[29] Bullinger's conception of the Apocalypse, however, actually differed very little from that of Bale. He prefaced his sermons with a summary of Relevation which might have been written by Bale himself. According to Bullinger, St. John had shown:

> That Christ Jesus our Lord, will neuer fayle in his Church
> in earth, but will gouerne it with his spirite and worde,
> through thecclestiasticall [sic] ministery, notwithstanding
> yt the church itself, whilest it remaineth in in this worlde
> shall suffer many thinges, for professing Christ and the
> truthe of his Gospell. And it openeth welneere all and
> singular the euils that the Church shall suffer. . . .All
> the which thinges apperteyne to this ende, that all the
> chosen being sufficently warned before, and prouided for in
> all ages whilest this worlde shall indure, may with true
> faith alone, cleaue vnto Christ our redemer, king and high
> prieste, only and eternall, and purely syncerely professe
> hym, call vpon him, serue him in innocencie of lyfe, and
> patiently wayt for his commyng to Judgement to delyuer and
> saue the godly: But contrarywise, that they should dispise
> all superstitions and the worlde it selfe with those his
> sondrye religions, felicities and pleasures, and beware of
> all vngodlines. And chiefly that they should flee
> Antichrist which shall come in the ende of the world,
> vsurping to him selfe most uniustly the kingdome and
> Priesthod of Christ, & greuously persecuting the Church of
> Christ, euen to the last Judgement.[30]

---

[29]These sermons were translated into English in 1561. That same year Bishop Parkhurst of Norwich wrote to Bullinger, "I have given directions to all the minsters of the Word throughout Suffolk and Norfolk, to procure either in Latin or English your sermons on the Apocalypse. For John Daws, a good and learned man and schoolmaster in the Town of Ipswich, has translated them into our mother tongue." I am indebted to a notation on the flyleaf of Yale University's copy of this work for this reference.

[30]Henrich Bullinger, A Hundred Sermons vppon the Apocalipse of Iesu Christ, trans. John Daws (London, 1573), preface.

For Bullinger as well as for Bale, St. John's vision was "an abridgement of hystories from Christes tyme, vnto the worldes end," which comforted the elect by showing that "all thynges are done by Gods prouidence, and that all euils and miseries shall come to an ende."[31] History was the manifestation of God's will, and as such it displayed a consistency--particularly for those who interpreted it with the aid of Revelation. Though the church must be prepared for "perils, calamities, contentions, troubles, sects, and persecutions" in every age, the saints knew that sooner or later--and in Bullinger's eyes probably sooner--Antichrist would finally be destroyed. In the meantime God had commanded His people to flee from antichristian rule, "not by bodely remeouing, but vnlikenes of maners."[32] Bullinger too correlated the binding of Satan and the millennial rule of Christ with the preaching of the Word for a thousand years after the Ascension. "For the preachyng of the Gospell was not in hucker mucker, but most cleare and manifest, nor short and pinched, but publyshed by the space of a thousand yeares."[33] When the millennium had ended sometime between 1034 and 1073, the Devil had been loosed--only to be opposed by the Waldensians, Wyclif, Huss, and so forth. But even though this loosing had initiated the last age--Bullinger constantly referred to his contemporaries as men "whom the endes of the world haue ouertaken"--it differed little from preceding ages. "For euermore, and in all ages haue sprang vp some holy and learned men, which beyng illumined and comforted of God, lyke Enoch and Jehe, haue resisted the vngodly and vngodlynes, and haue mainteyned the true Religion, wherby mens consciences that were afflicted by Antichrist haue receiued comfort."[34] Wyclif, Huss, and Jerome of Prague, and the sixteenth-century reformers as well, were merely continuing an ancient tradition.

---

[31] Ibid., 6.

[32] Ibid., 246.

[33] Ibid., 267.

[34] Ibid., 272.

Bullinger's sermons were by no means the last work on the Apocalypse to which the English were exposed during the Reformation By the end of Elizabeth's reign, at least ten commentaries on Revelation had appeared in English--including one by the future King James I and another by John Napier, the famous mathematician. More and more men--the great majority of them scholars and clergymen--were trying their hand at correlating the prophecies of St. John with the events of history. Convinced that they were living in the last age of the world, they hastened to expound the mysterious and obscure vision which was "a Comfortable and Necessary Discourse, for these Miserable and Daungerous Dayes." In so doing, they inevitably and perhaps consciously reinforced the ideas which the Book of Martyrs was spreading on a more popular level. Certainly by the end of the Elizabethan age the English people were well on their way to being convinced that they were a chosen people appointed by God to lead the world in repudiation of Antichrist and all his works. As William Haller has put it:

> The idea of a predestined salvation reserved for the elect,
> of the Church as a communion of elect souls beset in all
> ages by enemies without and within, of the progression of
> the elect from age to age towards an apocalyptical
> vindication--these conceptions assumed in many minds a
> meaning and an application which went beyond their merely
> religious context. . . . For the Church as they conceived it
> appeared now as one with the nation, and for many, besides
> the champions of a still more perfect reformation, the
> nation itself assumed something of the nature of a mystical
> communion of chosen spirits, a peculiar people set apart
> from the rest of mankind.[35]

This complex of ideas, which the early reformers were so successful in implanting in the minds of the Elizabethans, has generally been associated with the Puritans--particularly with those of them who went to America. As Haller has shown, it was in fact common property. The truth is that Puritanism, "growing

---

[35]Haller, 244-45.

up" in the midst of these ideas, probably received as much from as it contributed to the conception of an elect nation and its various concomitants. But at the same time it is also true that the Puritans differed from their contemporaries and eventually differed enough to emigrate to a wilderness and to fight a civil war. What they differed about, as everyone knows, was the nature of church polity, and it is important to note here that on this point the Puritans disagreed with Calvin too. For Calvin, as we have seen, felt that church polity should conform within certain limits to the changing requirements of each age. How and where the Puritans came by their conception of an eternally true and hence mandatory church polity will not be our primary concern. Recent scholarship has suggested that the Puritans may have been much more strongly influenced by Bucer, Peter Martyr, Zwingli, Bullinger, etc. than by Calvin.[36] Be that as it may, for our purposes it is sufficient to note that the Puritans as well as their English brethren were at one with Calvin in their Augustinian assumption that the goal toward which history was progressing--the establishment of the Kingdom of God--was and always had been present within the very fabric of history itself. History was nothing but the story of the Kingdom on earth, and this was why one could study history in prophecy and vice versa.

Millennialists, who could see no relationship between temporal and relative history and the absolute Judgment which was to destroy it, had no compunctions about sweeping away existing structures of church and society in the name of Kingdom come. But because they believed God nurtured His Kingdom within history, neither Calvin nor the Puritans nor their Anglican opponents were prepared to try to separate it from its matrix prematurely. Instead they were imbued with a strong compulsion to work--as God's instruments--for the transformation of church and society into an approximate and temporary image of the heavenly Kingdom. At this point their disagreements began, for all of them and all of their contemporaries too had different ideas as to how closely commonwealth and church could or should be fashioned in the heavenly image. There was much controversy

---

[36]See Leonard J. Trinterud, "The Origins of Puritanism," Church History, XX (March, 1951), 37-57.

over this among the Puritans themselves; but their solutions, while various, one and all presupposed the apocalyptic conception of history which their predessors had made so popular.

Chapter II.

THE EVOLUTION OF THE MILLENNIUM

Millennial ideas, as everyone knows, tend to be dangerously explosive. Given the right conditions, they frequently result in a radical drive to remake society or at least to give vent to old frustrations. William Haller has quite rightly pointed out that apocalyptic thinking in sixteenth-century England "led not to the pursuit of a millennium but to the aspiration after nationality, not to the expection of a messiah out of the blue but to the idea of an hereditary monarch called by the grace of God to rule the realm and defend the faith, not to the desire to cast down the mighty but to the resolution to cast out the interloper."[1] Nevertheless, while the Elizabethans were content to vest their apocalyptic aspirations in the creation of a Protestant England, many of the next generation demanded that England be made Puritan as well as Protestant. These men as well as their predecessors were driven by apocalyptic urgings. The apocalyptic ideas which had been expounded so vividly by men like Foxe and Bale were soon hitched to a much more extreme conception of the need for reformation than either of them had held. In the process the apocalyptic ideas themselves were changed little by little into a more radical type of millennial thinking, which in its own turn naturally reinforced the demand for further reformation.

One of the first men to give an undeniably Puritan interpretation to the apocalyptic scheme of history set forth by Bale and Foxe was Thomas Brightman, a scholarly clergyman who greatly admired the Genevan mode of reformation. Born in 1562, Brightman took B.A., M.A., and B.D. degrees from Cambridge, where he also was elected a fellow of Queens' College. In 1592, the year after he received his B.D. degree, he became rector of Haunes in Bedfordshire, where he lived quietly until his death in 1607. A celebrated preacher, who made no secret of his desire for futher reformation, Brightman's greatest contribution to the Puritan movement lay in his biblical exegesis, particularly his interpretation of the Apocalypse. Brightman spent his life studying the apocalyptic prophecies of the Scripture, and his writings--which were published abroad

---

[1]Haller, 62.

posthumously--consist almost entirely of commentaries on these
prophecies. By far the largest and most impressive is the one
on Revelation--<u>Apocalypsis Apocalypseos</u>--which he claimed to
have written with divine inspiration.[2] Certainly it gives
little indication of reliance on any other sources, although in
the light of his Genevan leanings, it is perhaps significant
that he used as his text the edition of the New Testament
prepared by Theodore Beza, Calvin's successor at Geneva.

After its first publication in 1609, Brightman's commentary
on the Apocalypse went through several editions both in Latin
and in English translation, including nine editions between 1641
and 1644 of an extract sometimes called <u>Brightman's Predictions
and Prophesies</u>. It was by far the most influential of his
writings, and its popularity with Puritan scholars is
undeniable. Virtually all of them who wrote on the Apocalypse
cited it at one point or another, if only to refute his
interpretations. John Cotton once wrote that "his paines have
been most serviceable to the Church of all that have written of
this Book [Revelation], and God is to be exceedingly magnified
for him, and his Learning esteemed; that having such a
Prophetical spirit, he spake so homely and plainly."[3]

It is not hard to see what attracted men of John Cotton's
views to Brightman's exegesis of the Apocalypse, for in it
Brightman did the same thing for Puritanism that Bale had done
for the English Reformation. He put it in historical
perspective. Just as Bale a generation earlier had discovered
in the Apocalypse historical justification for England's break
with the Catholic Church, so Brightman found there support for
the Puritan idea that there existed only one divinely ordained
form of church government. The differences between their two
interpretations indicate the distance Puritans had come along
the path of reform.

---

[2]James Mew, "Thomas Brightman," <u>Dictionary of National
Biography</u>, ed. Leslie Stephen and Sidney Lee, II (1949-50),
1247.

[3]<u>An Exposition upon the Thirteenth Chapter of the
Revelation</u> (London, 1655), 87.

Both men interpreted the Apocalypse as a history of the true
church in this world, "the story of Christ's Kingdom," but
whereas Bale had looked for the perfection of the Kingdom only
within the hearts of the elect, Brightman also found it in the
maintenance of a purer institutional discipline. For Bale the
true church on earth was embodied simply in the regenerate lives
of the faithful, its true form apparent to God alone. For
Brightman the true church existed wherever and whenever God's
ordinances were practised in their original purity.

Their different viewpoints can be seen by comparing their
commentaries on the fourth chapter of St. John's vision. Both
considered it to be a revelation of the eternal nature of God's
Kingdom.[4] In Bale's paraphrase St. John, ascending to heaven
and beholding God's throne, is moved to the consideration that
"no where else reigneth God but among his chosen people. He
dwelleth not in temples made by hand, he resteth not in houses
of man's preparation. Is the kingdom of God anywhere else than
within man? Hath God any temple that he more favoureth than
man's faithful heart?"[5] With these thoughts in mind Bale
interpreted the saints and the elders, the four beasts and the
glassy sea as types of the individual saint and his relationship
to God.

---

[4]Revelation 4 describes St. John's ascent to heaven where
he saw a throne "set in heaven," around which were seated
twenty-four elders clothed in white with gold crowns on their
heads. Out of the throne came "lightenings and thunderings and
voices," and before it burned seven lamps. Also before the
throne was a "sea of glass," while all around and about it flew
four "beasts," resembling respectively a lion, a calf, a man,
and an eagle.

[5]Bale, 298.

Brightman, on the other hand, saw the chapter as a description setting forth the eternal form of the church for the benefit of ages to come:

> For inasmuch as the manyfold chances and notable changes of it were to be related [in the rest of the book], the fleeing of it away, the return of it againe, the faymed frends, the open enemyes, the counterfait and craftie Apostles that should set forth themselues vnder the colours of the Church, and many other things of the like nature wherewith it should be sorely annoyed were to bee foretold, it was necessary that first of all a certayne portraiture and resemblance should be drawn of that Church, . . .least through ignorance of her right forme and figure, wee should be lesse able to know which is shee.[6]

Brightman did not mean that any time in history a specific church had achieved complete purity. "Wee must not think, that any Congregation on earth is to be found of such absolute puritie & faultlesse perfection, as this Church is here described to be of, but that all the holy assemblyes of the elect are accounted such in Christ before God the Father, though much earthly dregges be sprinckled vpon and among them."[7] The description in Revelation had been put there as an example so that men could endeavor to make their earthly assemblies conform to the heavenly pattern.

According to Brightman, therefore, the fourth chapter of Revelation should be interpreted not only in terms of the individual's relationship with God but also in terms of the visible community of saints in this world. Brightman's primary focus through his entire work is on the communion of the elect in its earthly manifestations. He believed that the

---

[6]Thomas Brightman, The Revelation of S. Iohn, Illustrated with an Analysis and Scholions (3rd ed.; Leyden, 1616), 215-16.

[7]Ibid., 216.

relationship between the visible church and the invisible
Kingdom was much closer than men had heretofore realized.
Whereas Bale had flatly denied that the Kingdom could be
identified with any visible church and Calvin had felt that the
relationship between Kingdom and church on earth was ambiguous
at best, Brightman unequivocally correlated the reign of Christ
with the enforcement of a specific kind of church
government--Presbyterian--and proceeded to interpret the
Apocalypse accordingly. Tracing out the story of Christ's
Kingdom on earth, he endeavored to show that the spiritual,
invisible community which was the true church did at certain
crucial points in time correspond to a great extent with the
visible, corporate church of this world.

This theme was established at the very beginning of his work
on the Apocalypse in his commentary on the first three
chapters. These chapters, which consist of letters addressed to
churches in seven cities of Asia Minor, Brightman believed to be
a description of "the vniuersall condition of the Church" from
the earliest times until the second advent. Each of the seven
cities was to be interpreted as the type of one of the various
churches which existed in the ages after Christ. By matching up
descriptions of these types with their anti-types or
"Counterpaynes," men could discover which historical church had
achieved the greatest purity in doctrine, worship, and
government and model their own churches accordingly.

The first of these cities was Ephesus and corresponded to
the first Christian church lasting from the preaching of the
Apostles until the time of Constantine the Great. This church
was one of great purity which combined true doctrine, holiness
of manners, and wholesome discipline. Its ministers spared no
trouble in teaching or in exercising discipline, not hesitating
to excommunicate any who should "offend the Church with his
naughtines." Here, if anywhere, the Kingdom had manifested
itself in visible form. "But godlines languisheth by litle and
litle, vnles it be continually blown vp and so kindled; and
often-times a certayne naked profession remayneth, where all the
force of it is starke dead, and lyeth quiet put out; as wee
shall presently see it fell out there with this church."[8]

---

[8]Ibid., 60.

Ephesus' godliness did indeed languish and from the heights upon which it stood, it was a surprisingly short way to the depths of depravity. Smyrna, the second city, typified the church during its headlong descent, a period lasting from the time of Constantine until the time of Gratian (about 382).

To Pergamus fell the dubious honor of representing the church in its period of utmost darkness and corruption (382 to 1300). Even during this time the light of truth was not entirely extinguished, for a few of the faithful--undismayed by "Romish tyranny"--held fast to sound doctrine. Then, when things looked darkest, the forerunners of the Reformation appeared: "Certayne Godly men, who did openly preach, that Antichrist was come, that holy dayes to Saints, Church-broken musicke, prayers for the dead, Pilgrimages, oyle, chrisme and such other things were all matters full of superstition."[9] These men were joined about 1120 by the Waldensians, Albigensians, and other reformers. From that time forth the war against Antichrist was waged with continually increasing vigor and success.

As far as Brightman was concerned, though, the Reformation proper began with the church of Thyatira (1300-1520), the church of Wyclif, Huss, and Jerome of Prague to name only a few. Just as individual saints grew in righteousness throughout their lives, so this church grew in holiness under the efforts of its reformers. "It is an excellent commendation to grow in godlines, and to exceed the former times of our life in the fruitfullnes of good workes, as wee grow towards our latter dayes. . . .So this Church all wayes increasing with a more ample progresse, did daily waxe great & strong of small beginnings."[10] Nor was this age notable for holiness alone. God "poured out vpon these selfe same tymes, such rich store of all gifts, as he did neuer elswhere in these last dayes."[11] Chief among these was the wonderful art of printing, which aided scholars' inquiries into "liberall learning" and thus helped

---

[9] Ibid., 92.

[10] Ibid., 100.

[11] Ibid., 121.

prepare the way for the deeper penetration of the next age into
the mysteries of salvation. The discoveries of the next age
were great indeed; after Thyatira came Sardis, Martin Luther's
church. Brightman considered Sardis to be the first truly
reformed church. It was the first one to make a clean break
with Rome and it also removed many popish errors. For all its
progress in the direction of reformation, "yet as touching the
Sacrament of the Supper, shee stucke as it were in the mire of
the corporall presence."[12] Further advances had to be made by
the next church, that of Philadelphia.

This church was the second truly reformed church to spring
up and corresponded to the church of Geneva, Huguenot France,
Holland, and Scotland. Here the divine power of Christ shone
forth in a special manner. There was no other place where
doctrine was more purely preached, the worship of God exercised
more uncorruptly, the diligence of the pastors more faithful, or
obedience more freely and willingly given by the people. The
thing that most impressed Brightman about the church of
Philadelphia was the quality of its discipline. Discipline, he
believed, was an important mark of a true church. No church
which failed to exercise it, especially excommunication, could
be accounted pure. By using its power of excommunication to
deny obstinate sinners entrance into the communion of the
godly--as had Ephesus--this church had achieved the enviable
state of true reformation. Brightman's emphasis on the
importance of excommunication in the work of reformation was not
merely the result of a desire to repress sinners. He also
thought of it as a prime method of conversion. Proper use of
excommunication brought purity to the church because it brought
salvation to men.

The Church of Philadelphia, wherein the ordinance of God was
in vigour of old, and is so at this day in the Counterpayne
of it, hath an vnlocked and opened dore, all reliques of
Antichrist being thrust out by the head and shoulders, but

---

[12]Ibid., 126.

most of all because the true vse of <u>excommunication</u> is
restored, whereby the gates of heauen are both shut and
opened, as also the dores of euery mans conscience are
vnsealed, that so Christ may come easily in without any
stay. For where there is a watch kept ouer the manners of
euery man, & men are admonished, reproued, cut of [off],
receiued in, as occasion is offered, and other things are
faithfully and diligently performed which the regard of the
saluation of euery one requireth; there all of the barres
and boltes of the heart are plucked away, and then indeed <u>do
the gates life [sic] up their heades that the King of Glory
may come in</u>.[13]

In the godly commonwealth of Geneva, Scotland, Holland, and
Protestant France, the discipline of the church was backed up by
the authority of the state. Minister and magistrate cooperated
to produce a godly people--each, however, working only within
his proper sphere. In this manner the keys to the Kingdom of
Heaven were held by minister and magistrate in conjunction, and
doors were thereby opened into the minds and hearts of their
fellow men. By thus coordinating the separate powers of church
and commonwealth in pursuit of the indivisible goal of holiness,
the best possible conditions for the regeneration of men had
been created in these reformed countries. The channels through
which the Spirit moved to bring the elect to their predestined
knowledge of grace were without obstacles. "And this is indeed
a most sweete societie, seeing the whole paynes and labour of
the ciuil Magistrate, ought to tend to this that <u>men might liue
with all godlines and honestie</u>."[14]

Godliness has its rewards, and the Philadelphians--according
to Revelation--were not to be without them. "Him that
overcometh will I make a pillar in the temple of my God, and he
shall go no more out: and I will write upon him the name of my
God, and the name of the city of my God, which is New
Jerusalem." (Rev. 3:12) This verse, commonly interpreted as a
prediction of the heavenly rewards awaiting individual saints,

---

[13]<u>Ibid.</u>, 201-202.

[14]<u>Ibid.</u>, 144.

Brightman applied instead to the entire community of
Philadelphians <u>within this world</u>. Philadelphians would enjoy
the felicities of New Jerusalem before the rest of God's elect,
not in heaven but on earth.

> But as touching this <u>new Ierusalem</u>, wee shall shew in the
> proper place, that it is not that <u>Citie</u> which the Saintes
> shall enioy in the Heauens, after this life, but that
> <u>Church</u>, that is to bee looked for vpon earth, the most noble
> and pure of all other, that euer haue been to that tyme.
> The rewards doe in a peculiar sort serue for the tymes
> but if this felicitie should be after the resurrection,
> it should bee common to all the Saints, not proper to
> this <u>Philadelphia</u>. This therefore doth signifie, both
> that the <u>Philadelphians</u> should endure vntill that
> restoring of the Church, wherein the <u>new Ierusalem
> shall come down from heaven, and shall converse with
> men</u>, as also that they shalbe ioyned with it in
> Couenant and societie, to bee endowed with the gift of
> that <u>heauenly Ierusalem</u> and to enjoy the same right and
> felicitie with it. At which tyme all men shall
> acknowledge, that they [Philadelphia's] reformation is
> not a devise of mans braine, as contentious brablers
> will needes haue it to bee, when they shall see the
> same ordinances to flourish in the <u>new Ierusalem</u>.[15]

The Philadelphians would not have long to wait for their
reward. Brightman predicted that they would enter New Jerusalem
within two hundred years of their church's first birth before
the beginning of the eighteenth century.

Philadelphia was only the sixth city mentioned in these
chapters of Revelation. Laodicea was the seventh and Brightman
naturally found the counter-type for this city in the Church of
England. Unfortunately, though, the English Laodicea had not
reached an even greater degree of reformation than had the
church of Philadelphia. In Revelation Laodicea is described as
lukewarm, neither hot nor cold, and the application of this
description to the Church of England was only too clear. "It is
not cold, in asmuch as it doth professe the sound, pure, and

---

[15]<u>Ibid.</u>, 155.

sincere doctrine of saluation, by which wee haue renounced that
Antichrist of Rome, and are risen out of that death as cold as
yce wherein wee lay before. But hott it is not, as whose
outward regiment is as yet for the greatest parte Antichristian
& Romish. In the degrees of clergie men, in elections &
ordinations, & the whole administration of the
Church-censures."[16] This was particularly distressing in a
nation so signally blessed by God. For more than forty years
God had poured forth a great abundance of all good things upon
England. He had given the English a queen, "so excelling in all
things that are praise-worthy, as the like to her no age euer
saw."[17] He had given the nation peace--that prime
prerequisite for the prosperity and well-being of any country.
Learning flourished; riches increased; fields abounded with corn
and cattle; cities grew; and above all, justice reigned. "What
neede many words?"[18] In addition to its material benefits
England had been blessed with skillful pastors and teachers, who
had preached the gospel of salvation purely and sincerely.
Though the nation's Antichristian enemies had raged and stormed,
they had been powerless to inflict harm upon the country. Truly
England had prospered beyond all former measure.

It was, however, this very prosperity that was responsible
for the backward state of English religion. "The plentie
therefore of all things for the mayntayning of this life, begat
this lukewarmenes. Neither is it strange that prosperitie
should closely steale away the mindes of men and draw them away
from God. It is often commaunded in the law that they should

---

[16]Ibid., 168.

[17]Ibid., 161.

[18]Ibid., 162.

take heede to themselues, least when they were full, and cloyed
with Gods blessings through fullnes, they should forget the
Lord."[19] Unless the Church of England was prepared to restore
the ordinances of God--particularly excommunications--to their
primitive purity, the nation could expect judgment according to
its sins. It was time for men to cease their profitless
argument and endless contention over religion and apply
themselves to remedying the defects of church discipline. After
all, many excellent preachers had labored for years that their
brethren might understand the truth. "What remayneth now but
that hee [Christ] should at length bring forth, his roddes
quickly to chasten those, whom hee hath been so long in
conuincing without any fruit or profit."[20]

The forthcoming judgment with which Brightman threatened his
recalcitrant brethren was no mere physical calamity, no piddling
seven years of lean kine to compensate for seven years of fat
ones. The great and lamentable calamity England should expect
would be apocalyptic in nature and one that would be shared by
all peoples not conforming to the Philadelphia model of purity.
As we have seen, Brightman believed the world was upon the verge
of entering the age of the New Jerusalem. In such an age
nations which refused to conform to the requirements of the
godly could only expect unprecedented devastation, indeed
destruction, from the forces of righteousness.

All of this would seem to suggest that Brightman was
predicting the advent of the millennium in a manner not far
removed from that of John of Leyden. It is true that Brightman
believed that the reign of Christ in His Kingdom (the church)
would manifest itself _visibly_ on this earth for a thousand
years. But it is also true that he thought of this
manifestation as appearing in a gradual fashion within rather
than without history. At the time he wrote his commentary on
Revelation, he considered the millennium to have been in
existence for three hundred years. Like Bale, Brightman

---

[19]_Ibid._, 173.

[20]_Ibid._, 199.

did not believe that the thousand-year bondage of Satan was to take place in the future. The binding of the Devil had begun in 300 and ended in 1300. Thereafter he had ranged once more in the world, opposed at the same time by the ever growing light of the truth. The elect had flocked to the gospel wherever it had been preached truly and purely, "which eger desire and endeauour of theirs is called the first resurrection."[21] St. John's prophecy that the saints should reign with Christ for a thousand years had already begun to be fulfilled at the time of Wyclif and the earliest reformers. Every day truth was gaining in strength and power, and Brightman was sure that it would continue to do so until "Christ shall haue reigned from some Ages most gloriously vppon earth, by ministery of his Seruants."[22] This last phrase is an important one. The rule of Christ did not mean that the Saviour would appear in visible form. It meant, rather, that the church would be advanced "vnto the highest honour that can be, euen aboue all Empire that is."[23] The millennium Brightman envisaged was simply a world in which religion took precedence over all other considerations.

Even though much progress had been made toward this ideal world, several prophecies still had to be accomplished. The Jews had to be converted, Rome and the Turks destroyed, and the Reformation completed before Christ could truly be said to rule the world. Brightman thought all of these things would occur before the end of the seventeenth century, but he did not think they would be followed by the Last Judgment. By the year 1700 there would still be another six hundred years to go before the millennium was up and even then, according to Brightman, the Day of Judgment might not come.[24] He considered those who were so venturous "as to set down a certaine yeare and day almost of the

---

[21]Ibid., 1047.

[22]Ibid., 1051.

[23]Ibid.

[24]Brightman thought there might be another thousand-year period after this first one for the special benefit of the converted Jews.

last iudgement," to be greatly deceived in their own powers.[25]

To sum up, then, Brightman believed that the millennium had begun with the Reformation--properly dated, as he and his contemporaries thought, from 1300--and had spread gradually across Europe as the reforming spirit moved from nation to nation. It was now about to enter its greatest period of glory with the conversion of the Jews (in 1650) and the destruction of Rome and the Turks. Its full establishment within the bounds of history would be marked by the subjection of the whole world to the rule of the Church. "At this time, all nations shalbe at the Churches command, & that at a becke, requiring & taking lawes & ordinances from it whereby they may be gouerned."[26] This church--to which the Philadelphians would be joined in "Couenant and societie"--would be one of utmost purity:

No man shalbe gathered into this Church, but he onely that shalbe among those that haue been chosen from euerlasting, to eternall life. How notable shall the glory be of this Church, which shall not be defiled at all with any hypocrites & counterfaite Christians, as it was wont to fare with the Church of old. How goodly a feild [sic] to see to, will this be, that shalbe laden with a most plentifull Croppe of good corne cleane rid of all Tares, Cockell and darnell? . . . It may fall out, that some men may slippe sometimes thorough humaine infirmity, but holy admonitions, and wholesome Discipline, purely & faithfully exercised, shall bring them home againe in time to repentance, and good conversation.[27]

When the light of truth had spread to its predestined bounds, the church would be composed only of the elect. Until that time came, though, men could best continue the work of purification by restoring discipline to its right and proper place in church government. Unless England did just that, Brightman warned his compatriots, their country would be

---

[25]Brightman, 1053.

[26]Ibid., 1019.

[27]Ibid., 1074-1075.

excluded from the reign of the saints. Only by conforming to the model so clearly set up in the second reformed church in Geneva, Holland, Scotland, and France could the English people be assured of a place in New Jerusalem.

Brightman's commentary on the Apocalypse was first published in 1609. Three years later a Scotsman published a commentary on St. John's vision which was also destined to become influential in Puritan circles. This commentary, however, largely ignored the question of church polity. Perhaps because it did so, its author, Patrick Forbes, eventually became a bishop in the Scottish church. Forbes, who was born in 1564, studied theology at the Universities of St. Andrews and Glasgow and spent some time at Oxford and Cambridge, though he apparently never took a degree. He was offered the chair of divinity at St. Andrews; but preferring to pursue his studies privately, he refused and retired to his family estates at Corse. There his friends and neighbors pressed him to make use of his abilities in preaching. Eventually, though not ordained, Forbes began to give occasional sermons. When King James ordered him to stop, however, he submitted at once. Finally, he was ordained in 1611 and shortly thereafter became the minister at Keith.

Forbes' views on the increasingly divisive questions of church order are hard to determine. A year before he was ordained, he had supported the group which unsuccessfully opposed the introduction of a moderate episcopacy in Scotland. Nevertheless its introduction caused no schism in his church at Keith, and only a few years later in 1618 he was consecrated bishop of Aberdeen. When the King introduced practices such as kneeling into the church that same year, Forbes made it plain he considered them to be matters of indifference and went along with the new orders without protest. He does not, however, seem to have been deeply attached to episcopalian polity. When Charles I attempted to make Scotland's church conform to the English pattern, Forbes strenuously opposed him until he suffered a stroke in 1632. He died three years later.[28] In view of Forbes' career, it is difficult to decide just what his ideas on church polity were. If, on the one hand, he opposed the episcopacy, he apparently did not feel strongly enough about

---

[28]George W. Sprott, "Patrick Forbes," DNB, VII, 407-409.

did not feel strongly enough about it not to become a bishop
himself. Yet, on the other hand, after becoming a highly
regarded bishop in the Scottish church, he strenuously
opposedfurther conformity to English church polity. No doubt in
an age before denominational lines had begun to develop, he felt
that within certain boundaries the forms of church government
were much less important than the ministry of God's Word. At
least this seems to have been his attitude when he wrote his
commentary on Revelation.

Like virtually all his contemporaries, Forbes was convinced
that Revelation foretold the complete history of the church.

In this prophecie, is the whole mischiefe, in the parties,
their practises, the Church, her condition thereby, God his
manifold wrath thereupon, to the full overthrow at length of
all the enemies, and deliuerance of his Church; so at large
and cleerely set forth, as we are not onely now to beleeue
the things told vs before, because they are already in a
great part come to passe: but also, by the cleere light here
opened to see what yet resteth to be performed.[29]

When it came to correlating St. John's prophecies with
actual historical events, Forbes was considerably less specific
than many other commentators. This was largely because he
thought of the prophecies as _types_ of events rather than as
descriptions of particular occurences. For example, he
interpreted the four horsemen of the Apocalypse as types of the
spread of the gospel and the judgments of God upon the world for
"the Gospel persecuted."[30] The white horse symbolized the
preaching of the Gospel, the red horse war, the black horse
famine, and the pale horse pestilence.

---

[29]Patrick Forbes, _An Learned Commentarie Vpon the
Revelation of Saint Iohn_ (2d ed.; Middelburg, 1617), "The Author
to the Christian Reader."

[30]The vision of the four horsemen is contained within the
opening of the first four of the seven seals, Rev. 6: 1-8.

Forbes did not believe that the vision of the four horsemen
represented all of the evangelism, war, famine, and pestilence
which would occur throughout the history of the church. Rather
the four horsemen referred to a particular period--the time of
the preaching of the Gospel under the Roman Empire--and had to
be interpreted as such.

Forbes was inclined to tread a middle ground, just as he was
in matters of polity. Interpreters of Revelation, he felt,
should be careful of "iumbling Seales, Trumpets and Vials, to
the confusion of al order, and light of Story, which in this
Prophesie is most orderly set downe, with speciall relation to
distinct euents." But it was absurd to suppose that the visions
were "so many knots or periods of time exactlie cutted, within
which, the accommodation of each is to bee sought."[31]
Revelation described the history of the church, but only in
broad outline. The "distinct euents" which it prophesied were
not so much particular historical occurences as they were
spiritual events which had consequences in history. A good
example of this kind of interpretation is Forbes' commentary on
the meaning of the seven trumpets.[32] These he thought
described the gradual rise of Antichrist within the church. He
correlated each of them with the "events" which had brought
about this rise. The first such event or trumpet was the
appearance of self-love and contention in the church,
which in turn led to the advent of superstition. "The first
decay was of Religion, in the heartes & liues of men. This
second, is in the ordinary worship, which in great part now
becommeth corrupted; & therby, a great part both of common
professours and Pastors, become dead in superstition."[33]
After the corruption of common worship came the fall of "great
and learned Pastors" from the truth and the true church; and
then under the fourth trumpet the world succumbed to "grosse
ignorance in a great part, darkening all true knowledge"

---

[31]Forbes, 39.

[32]Rev. 8, 9 and 11:15-19.

[33]Forbes, 61.

including "humane sciences and liberall arts."[34] The first
four trumpets had conditioned the world for Antichrist. Under
the fifth he rose to the full height of his iniquity, sending
out hordes of locust-like clergy to plague the people. The
sixth trumpet, the Mohammedan armies, was a judgment of God upon
the iniquities of Antichrist and at the same time a preparation
for his overthrow. Under this trumpet began the preaching of
the Gospel which would ultimately result in the triumph of
Christ over His enemy. "[Christ] fitteth apt instruments, who
by diuine motion, studying diligently the Scriptures, preach
euery where the Gospel. So, as by the true rule rightly
applied, the true Church of God is discerned from the false: and
light growing, Antichrist his kingdome is in a degree, shaken,
and beginneth to fall: and in the seuenth Trumpet is vtterly and
for euer destroied."[35]

Forbes' overall conception of the history of the church,
then, was one in which changes in its condition occurred
gradually, usually as a result of the cumulative effect of
various spiritual alterations. In this manner the church moved
in history toward a final vindication, progressing through
periods of persecution, of corruption, of light and truth. As
it approached the time of its deliverance from the hands of its
enemies, knowledge of the truth grew continually. "The increase
of light & grace towards the Church, shall continue, till
Antichrist being ouerthrowne, and the Iewes ioining to the
faith: she inioie a gracefull and peaceable state heere, as a
Bride prepared for her husband. This to be the minde of the
Holy Ghost, the whole course of this Prophesie sheweth
euidently."[36]

At this point Forbes with his emphasis on the historical
progress of Gospel truth toward an ultimate vindication--begins
to sound rather like Thomas Brightman. His ideas were very
similar to those of his predecessor. Nevertheless Forbes' lack
of concern over problems of discipline and polity made his

---

[34]Ibid., 64.

[35]Ibid., 81.

[36]Ibid., 85.

emphases vary somewhat from Brightman's at several points. Of these perhaps the most important was the whole question of the relationship of the church and Kingdom in history. Forbes addressed this question very directly in his commentary, since one of his main concerns was to refute the Catholic contention that the Protestant church had not existed before Luther. Rather than undertaking to furnish detailed documentary evidence for the existence of "protestants" throughout the history of the church after the manner of John Foxe, Forbes chose to refute the Catholics on the crucial point of the relationship between Christ's Kingdom and the historical church or, to put it in his words, "the true militant church of Christ vpon earth" and "the visible church."

He began to discuss this problem in his commentary upon the fourth chapter of Revelation. He too thought this chapter set forth a type of the true church "for stablishing of the heart of Iohn and al Christians, against the manifold dangers, wrestlings, decayes, and apparent eclipses of the Church" in the course of the subsequent story.[37] According to Forbes, the throne seen by St. John represented the rule of God in the church, while the twenty-four elders surrounding it were the elect. The three dispensations of grace toward the church--the Spirit, the Word, and the ministry of the Word--were symbolized respectively by the seven lamps, the glassy sea, and the four beasts. "Thus haue we the type of the true militant church of Christ vpon earth, but heauenly, such as alwayes, by powerful protection, and gracious dispensation of his Spirit, Word and Ministrie thereof, hee hath preserued in the greatest power of darkenes."[38] For Forbes, therefore, these three dispensations of grace were the marks by which the true church could be distinguished in this world; and insofar as any visible church manifested them, it partook of Christ's rule. It was

---

[37]Ibid., 10.

[38]Ibid., 19.

here that Forbes differed most significantly from Brightman.
Brightman considered discipline--exercised by means of a
particular church polity--to be one of the essential marks of
the true church. Forbes, on the other hand, made no reference
at all to discipline in connection with the true church, nor
indeed did he refer to it at length anywhere in his commentary.
For him the essence of the church was not discipline but the
Spirit's re-creation or regeneration of the lives of men through
the ministry of the Word. The faithful preaching of the Word
therefor constituted the true reformation of antichristian
corruption in the church. It was only through such preaching
that the Spirit could operate. "In this last reuiuing of the
Gospell, the word should be cleare and pure as at the first, and
accompanied with the force of the spirit: yet the dispensation,
donation, and operation of the holy Ghost should not bee in that
[miraculous] manner, but should bee mingled with the word: the
spirit and vertue thereof, accompanying the preaching of the
Gospell; . . . with the word and by the word preached, the
spirit should worke in the Saints."[39]

   Clearly Forbes believed that the true church, the Kingdom of
Christ, existed within history. In spite of the fact that he
did not link its existence to a specific church polity, Forbes
did believe that Christ's Kingdom was visible on earth. The
bishop of Aberdeen did not agree with Bale's definition of the
Kingdom within history as "the hidden congregation of the
faithful." He was fully prepared to admit that in some sense
the true church had been hidden during the ascendancy of
Antichrist. This was an important point in his refutation of
the Catholics. Yet because for him the church militant was not
only Christ's reign in the hearts of His elect but the
conjunction of the Spirit and the ministry of the Word, Forbes
could not dissociate the true church from the visible church.
He maintained that "no way euer was or shall be to become a
member of the true Church, but by comming through the visible
Church."[40] But if the true church necessarily had to be part
of the visible church, then Forbes was left with the problem of
justifying separation from the Catholic Church, the only

---

[39] Ibid., 145.

[40] Ibid., 132.

visible church on earth for so many centuries. His answer was simple enough:

> The true Church in Antichrist his greatest preuayling, was alwaies within his compasse, within which, all were euer accounted to be his owne, but yet were not. As within the compasse of the holy Citie, and Court of the Temple, were the Temple and witnesses in it, Chapter 11. besides, as no way could be to the Temple, but through the Citie and Court: . . . .[But] at length [Antichrist's] impietie came to that height by murthering the Saintes, that it was said to them, Come vp hither, and so a visible separation was made, not from the church, but from the thiefe and Traitor in the Church."[41]

This then, was the reason why the Catholic Church, for all its visibility could lay no claim to be the true church.

> Heere is the fallacie, that by aequiuocation they [the Catholics] conclude, if the Church hath alway beenevisible, then are we the true Church. Here more is added. For albeit the Church be always visible, yet the truth and true professors in it are not always so. . . The true Church is in some sort euer visible, though not in her selfe, yet in infallible Ensignes, as who seeth the Citie and Court, he seeth in a sort the Temple, because albeit hee see it not distinctly, yet seeing the Citie and Court, hee is certaine that the Temple is there. So seeing the visible Church, within whose compasse, though no eye see them: yet God hath his true worshippers, one seeth also the true Church. For within the Church are truth and lies, Christ and Antichrist, and either of them now and then obtaine in it, and hold place communiter in toto, but neuer vniuersaliter in singulis.[42]

Within history Christ and Antichrist were in constant conflict in the visible church and would be until Christ finally triumphed. If the visible church would never be totally good or totally evil before Christ's second coming, neither would its

---

[41]Ibid.

[42]Ibid., 133.

state in this world be one of equilibrium. As we have seen,
Forbes believed that by means of God's providence it was
constantly moving toward an ultimate goal, i.e., resurrection
and redemption. The iniquities of Antichrist, far from blocking
this eschatological progress, had materially contributed to it
by calling forth the God-given energies of the elect in
resistance. It was not only "the impietie" of Antichrist that
had brought the true church out of its previous hiding; it was
also the impact of a "plentiful dispensation of spirituall
graces from heauen."[43] When the Word of God was effectually
felt in the hearts of the elect, they could not long remain
unheard in this world. "Who can restraine the breach of Great
waters? what congealed cloude can keepe in thunder? and,
excessiue ioy, a heart, of any thing, can least hold vp. Forth
therefore, this hid Church behoued to come . . . like the
Swelling of Iorden, like sonnes of thunder . . . like the
bursting out of a blythe heart, which cannot holde vp a surfet
of ioy."[44]

Forbes like Brightman, thought of the Reformation as a last
great preaching of grace by means of which the true church
militant would become visible upon earth--visible not by the
enforcement of discipline under a particular polity, but simply
in the ministry of the Word and the predestined response of the
saints to it. "Through the cleare light of the Gospell
preached, Antichrist being laide open, the hearts of God his
faithfull seruantes shall be filled with holy indignation and
zeale to imploy their power to God his honour, in his ouerthrow,
stirred thereto by the preachers of the truth."[45] When
Antichrist had been overthrown by "God his glorious and powerful
presence in his owne true Church opened and made visible,"[46] a
millennium of earthly bliss would begin for the church. Forbes'
interpretation of the millennium was quite similar to that of
Brightman. He too followed an Augustinian interpretation of
Satan's binding, placing it between 300 and 1300--after which

---

[43]Ibid., 126.

[44]Ibid., 128.

[45]Ibid., 148.

[46]Ibid., 149.

the Devil had been loosed to rage in antichristian fury against
the saints. He also thought that the first resurrection was the
spiritual resurrection of God's chosen from a life of sin. Yet,
like Brightman, he broke with the strictly Augustinian
interpretation of the millennium by placing the prophesied
period of the church's happiness in the future, not the past.

At this point, however, Forbes introduced a new element into
the interpretation of the millennium. Instead of interpreting
the day of judgment described in the Apocalypse as the Last
Judgment, he thought it referred to a kind interim judgment in
which the church's enemies would be condemned and sent to hell.
Since this judgment and consignment to hell would be final, the
church would never again have to suffer the persecutions of the
Dragon, the Whore, the Beast, and the false Prophet. The
millennium which their destruction would inaugurate would not be
one in which the church would achieve absolute perfection. "Wee
must not imagine that any such condition shall be, here in this
earth, that no hypocrite shall be within the Church."[47] It
would simply be a period prior to the final coming of Christ
during which the church would not be troubled by open corruption
and enmity.

When now the Whore, Beast, and Dragon, beeing destroyed, and
so, the Church freed both of couered deceiuers, and open
hostility, shee shall enioy quiet state in a plentifull
dispensation of light. Which condition, shall no more bee
interrupted againe, by any new foes, or loosing againe of
the Dragon (as after his first restraint) but shall continue
till she be translated from this state of grace, to the
state of glory in the heauens. So as now, vpon this second
taking of the Dragon, the Saintes shall not onely reigne and
liue a thousand yeeres, as in a sort they did, vpon his
first captiuity, but henceafoorth for euermore. And yet,
this goodly condition is not to bee so dreamed of, as if
henceafoorth the Church shall bee altogether free of all
euils: (which cannot fully fall here) but neuer againe, shal
either deceit of darknesse, or hostile inuasion, trouble
her. But her last euil, amidst plenty both of light and
peace, shall bee security. In which estate the Lord shall
find the world at his comming againe.[48]

---

[47]Ibid., 249.

[48]Ibid., 237-238.

Characteristically Forbes made no guesses about when the church would enter its period of millennial bliss. He would only say that Antichrist's downfall had already begun and that hence the beginning of the millennium could not be far off. But if Forbes would not speculate about such matters, there were plenty who would. One such person was Johann Heinrich Alsted (1588-1638), a Dutch Reformed theologian whose work on the millennium, <u>Diatribe de Mille Annis</u>, was cited by Puritan authors for more than half a century after its publication in 1627. Alsted was a famous teacher at Dutch universities and in the course of his career put together a series of compends in nearly every branch of knowledge. His book on the millennium, however, is quite short and was written specifically to defend the idea of a future period of earthly peace and well-being for the church.

Alsted, unlike Forbes, believed in correlating the prophecies of St. John with precise periods of time. In his interpretation of the Apocalypse, the vision of the seals lasted from the 94 to 606, i.e., from St. John's death to the reign of the emperor Phocas; the vision of the trumpets corresponded to the oppression of the church by the Popes between 606 and 1517; and the vision of the vials covered the period from 1517 to 1694 when the millennium would begin. Not only was Alsted prepared to predict the exact time of the millennium's commencement, he was sure that it would be inaugurated by nothing less than the bodily resurrection of all the martyrs who had died for the Christian faith. This interpretation of the first resurrection is radically different from the interpretations of the same event set forth by Bale, Brightman, and Forbes. They interpreted the first resurrection as the spiritual regeneration of the elect (rising from the death of sin to the life of the spirit) and correlated it with the binding of Satan during the thousand years stretching roughly from Constantine to Wyclif. The restraint of the Devil applied only to the invisible elect who, in spite of the great darkness of this period, did not succumb to antichristian corruptions. Although Alsted also correlated the binding of Satan with the first resurrection, he placed them both in the future--an interpretation much closer to radical pre-millennialism than those of his English predecessors.

According to him, there simply was no evidence that the Devil had yet been bound for a thousand years. "It cannot be proved out of any <u>History</u>."[49]

Not too surprisingly, Alsted had to spend a good deal of time defending himself against charges of being a chiliast, one who envisaged a period of carnal joys for the saints during the millennium. Alsted, however, specifically repudiated the idea of chiliasm. "In the same opinion we dislike, and disprove, That it allows carnal security, That it affirms that no ungodly men shall be remaining for those thousand years; That it maintains that Christ shall reign visibly here on earth."[50] His conception of the millennium was not one in which the church would attain a state of perfection here on earth. Christ would not appear to rule in person over his church, nor would the saints cease to be subject to sin and death.

> For neither shall the men, who for all that time shall live on earth, be so blessed, that either they themselves shall be voyd of sinnes, or separated from the company of sinners. It shall not be so. There shall be a great difference between the happinesse of thousand years, and that of everlasting life. The godly men then, (except the Martyrs) for the whole space of these thousand years, shall be subject both to sin and death, and shall have the wicked intermix't with them. But there shall be no such matter in the life Eternall.[51]

The millennium would be a period within history--"before the last day"--during which the church would enjoy the greatest degree of happiness possible for it on earth. The exact constituents of this happiness could be predicted:

---

[49] Heinrich Alsted, <u>Diatribe de Mille Annis</u>, translated as <u>The Beloved City or the Saints Reign on Earth a Thovsand Yeares</u> (London, 1643), 35.

[50] <u>Ibid.</u>, 71.

[51] <u>Ibid.</u>, 78-9.

> The happy estate of the Church in this life shall consist of
> the Resurrection of the Martyrs, and their kingdom here on
> earth; of the freedome of the Church from the persecution of
> the enemies of the Gospel, by an utter overthrow of them; of
> a lasting peace which shall arise from thence; of the
> encrease of the Church, or the multitude of the believers by
> the conversion of the Jews, and Nations not yet converted;
> of the Reformation of Doctrine, (or a greater enlightment)
> and life, among all estates of men; of the Majesty also, and
> great glory of the Church; and lastly, of the sincere joy
> thereof.[52]

Of these various constituents of Alsted's millennium
perhaps the most significant for our purposes is the reformation
of doctrine and life. It points to a concern for discipline and
godliness on his part which is very similar to that of
Brightman. For Alsted too the millennium represented a
continuation of the Reformation. In this sense it was an
integral part of the church's progress toward an eschatological
consummation. The Reformation was properly interpreted as mere
preparation for the advent of the millennium. "What the
condition of the Church hath been, and now is, since the yeer
1517, to this prsent [sic], is known unto us partly from
Histories, partly from our own notice, and remembrance. What it
shall be hereafter, . . .to the beginning of the 1000. yeers, we
cannot in particular determine. But this we know in generall,
That the Church is to be purged, purified, and cleansed, by this
persecution, which at this day it suffers; That by this means it
may be by little and little prepared for that great Reformation,
which the Epocha, or Account of those thousand yeers shall
bring.[53]

---

[52]Ibid., 33. Italicized in original.

[53]Ibid., 7.

Alsted was firmly convinced that this larger, millennial
reformation was to be preeminently a reformation of men's
lives. Some of his critics argued that since the fundamentals
of salvation were already clearly known, the church was
sufficiently reformed. No further reformation ought to be
expected. To these men Alsted reiterated that "the great
Reformation which we declare shall come to passe, shall concerne
matter of Life, as well as Doctrine."[54] The foundation of
doctrine would not be changed, though an end would be put to the
contentions "whereby the Body of Christ is torn in pieces."
Obscure places in the Scriptures would be more clearly and fully
understood during the millennium. Most important of all, the
lives of men would truly reflect godliness. The church, freed
from warfare with external enemies, would be able to concentrate
on "the Spiritual combate and wrestling, which, while it lives
here, it hath triall of from the lusts of the flesh."[55] Until
the church had done all that it could to bring the power of the
Spirit to bear upon the business of daily living, its work on
earth would not be finished; nor would history be ripe for its
consummation.

It should be clear by now that among the interpreters of the
Apocalypse we have examined there was a distinct development
toward a more radical interpretation of the millennium radical
in the sense that it differed sharply from the well-established
and generally accepted Augustinian conception of the thousand
years. Bale and Bullinger insisted upon the invisibility of the
true church on earth and thought of the millennium as the
thousand years when--in spite of the corruptions of the papal
Antichrist--the elect had enjoyed the invisible dominion of
Christ in their hearts. This for them had been the binding of
Satan. Brightman and Forbes, on the other hand, projected the
prophesied period of the church's felicity into the future and
related it to a gradual appearance of the true church on earth.
They too, however, placed the first resurrection and the
thousand years of Satan's binding in the past. Of all the
interpreters we have looked at, Alsted was the most radical

---

[54]Ibid., 79.

[55]Ibid., 76.

with his belief in the future binding of Satan and the bodily resurrection of the martyrs a thousand years before the Day of Judgment. This interpretation brought him closer to an extreme view of the millennium than any of his predecessors--extreme in this case defined as a conception of the millennium as a future state of absolute perfection for the church on earth, inaugurated by the advent of Christ and the bodily resurrection of the martyrs, and characterized by the absence of all evil and the personal reign of Christ with his saints. Neither Alsted nor any of the others conceived of the millennium as such an extra-historical period of other-worldly perfection. Unlike apocalyptic fanatics like John of Leyden, they stressed the existence of Christ's Kingdom in history. When they postulated a future millennium, they visualized it as a continuation and to a certain extent a culmination of the spiritual progress of the church in history. The millennium for them was to be a period during which the visible church would approach perfection, but not one in which it would actually arrive there. This would occur only after the Day of Judgment.

Up to 1627 the English had interpreted Revelation in relatively moderate terms. In that year, however, the English counterpart of Alsted's interpretation of the millennium was published. Ironically its author was an extremely shy and modest scholar who was probably not even a Puritan. Almost an exact contemporary of Alsted, Joseph Mede was born at Berden, Essex in 1586 of "Parents of honest rank."[56] He displayed a great talent for languages at an early age by learning Hebrew by himself. In 1602 he went to Christ College, Cambridge, where he was tutored for three years by Daniel Rogers, a non-conformist. Under suspicion for Puritan tendencies, Mede was nevertheless elected a fellow of Christ College in 1613 through the influence of Lancelot Andrews. Mede's ideas on church reformation are far from clear cut, though his sympathies seem to have been definitely Anglican. Writing to a Puritan correspondent about genuflecting before the alter, he confessed that:

> I have not been unacquainted with speculations in things of this nature: they were my eldest thoughts and studies, full twenty years ago, . . . before I was any proficient in the

---

[56]The Works of the Pious and Profoundly-Learned Joseph Mede, B.D., ed. John Worthington (London, 1672), i.

Apocalypse. And it may be I have had so many Notions that way as would have made another man a Dean or a Prebend or something else ere this. But the point of the <u>Pope's being Antichrist</u>, as a dead fly, marred the savour of that ointment. And besides I am no Practitioner nor active, but a Speculator only.[57]

Mede here seems to be saying that his inclinations were to retain such ceremonies, but that he was deterred by the thought that they might be antichristian. At any rate, he was correct in describing himself as a "Speculator" rather than a "Practitioner," for he passed the rest of his life as a fellow of Christ College and died there in 1638.

Mede published a number of works, but as in the case of Brightman his reputation was established by his work on the Apocalypse, in particular by his <u>Clavis Apocalyticae</u>. This commentary on Revelation soon gained and retained a widespread influence among students of St. John's vision, an influence which lasted well into the nineteenth century. No doubt one of the most important reasons for its popularity was Mede's concentration upon the inner coherence which he thought characterized the Apocalypse. It seems likely that he came to his conception of the millennium not so much from theological convictions about the nature of the church and its history as from his study of the text itself. As his seventeenth-century biographer John Worthington put it, "a man can hardly, without admitting it [i.e., a future millennium],

---

[57]<u>Ibid.</u>, 818. Mede's correspondent was William Twisse, later a member of the Westminster Assembly. His reply to Mede is an interesting commentary on the difficulties of defining the word "Puritan." "For sometimes I have been censured for a Puritan, sometimes for a good fellow; My preaching as in opposition to Popery was opportune to undergo the one censure before persons Popishly affected; and my free conversation in the enjoying of my friends (yet I thank God without all scandal) hath exposed me to the other, and that from the same mouths." <u>Ibid.</u>, 821. (Both letters were written in 1635.)

make good sense of those places in the 20 and 21 Chapters of the
<u>Revelation</u>, which tell us of a <u>First</u> and <u>Second Resurrection</u>,
and of a <u>Jerusalem descending out of Heaven from God</u>: Which last
(I have often heard our Author say) seemed to him extremely
harsh to expound of the State of Bliss in Heaven."[58]

Acting on the principle that the Apocalypse had an inner
coherence which could be discovered without attempting any
application of its prophecies to specific events, Mede prefaced
his commentary with "the Synchronisme and order of the
prophecies of the Revelation," or "Things to be fore-knowne" to
the interpreter. Mede believed that what might be called a
technique of literary criticism was the key to understanding
this difficult and obscure prophecy.

If the <u>Order</u>, <u>Method</u> and <u>Connexion</u> of the <u>Visions</u> be framed
and grounded upon supposed Interpretation, then must all
Proofs out of that Book needs be founded on begged
principles and humane conjectures: But on the contrary, if
the <u>Order</u> be first fixed and settled out of the indubitate
[sic] Characters of the letter of the Text, and afterward
the <u>Interpretation</u> guided, framed and directed by that
<u>Order</u>; then will the variety of the Expositions be drawn
into a very narrow compass, and Proofs taken from this Book
be evident and infallible, and able to convince the
Gain-sayers."[59]

Mede found a number of "synchronismes" in the prophecies of
Revelation which need not detain us here. His principal
innovation was to synchronize the vision of the seven seals and
the seven trumpets (Rev. 4 to Rev. 10:7) with the description of
the two beasts and the pouring out of the seven vials (Rev. 10:8
to end). The seals and the trumpets foretold "the successive
States and Changes of the Roman [i.e., secular] Kingdom," while

---

[58] <u>Ibid.</u>, ix.

[59] <u>Ibid.</u>, 581.

the two beasts and the vials described the history of the church
during the same period. Revelation could be divided into two
great parallel prophecies--one depicting secular history and
other sacred history--"until both do meet in one in Ecclesia
regnante, when all the Kingdoms of the world shall become the
Kingdoms of our Lord and of his Christ."[60] As we have
suggested, Mede's conception of this "Ecclesia regnante" or
millennium was very like that of Alsted. He too clearly and
unequivocally correlated the binding of Satan with the bodily
resurrection of the martyrs--though he thought the martyrs would
reign in heaven rather than earth--and placed these events in
the future. Like Alsted, he thought of this period as one of "a
most blissefull peace, and happy security from the hereticall
Apostasies and calamitous sufferings of former times" for the
church, and repudiated the idea that Christ would reign on earth
in person or that the (literally) unresurrected saints ruling
the world would be immortal.

But however closely Mede's ideas about the millenium
resembled those of Alsted, his conception of the true church and
its position in history was very unlike that of his Dutch
contemporary. Mede considered the true church to be "that holy
Society and Company of Believers, which as they accord and are
joyned together in one common Faith of all Divine Truths needful
to Salvation, so are they also free from the fellowship of such
enormous abominations and mortal errors as destroy and overturn
it."[61] The key phrase in this definition of the true church
is "enormous abominations and mortal errors." Mede, unlike some
of his more Puritan predecessors, thought that the fundamental
sin of Antichrist had been the worship of saints and relics or
more accurately belief in the mediation of saints,
since such a belief derogated from Christ's unique and sole
mediating position in the "Oeconomy of Redemption." If this
diagnosis of Antichrist's apostasy were correct, then the

---

[60]Ibid., 918.

[61]Ibid., 649. Italicized in original.

primary and perhaps the only reformation necessary in the
visible church was the elimination of the doctrine of the
mediation of the saints. The essence of the true church was
simply belief in the "Divine Truths needful to Salvation."
Noticeably this conception excluded not only the exercise of
discipline and the government of the church, but even the
ministry of the Word. Whatever may be said about the extent of
Mede's devotion to Anglicanism--and it may have been
considerable--he certainly was not a Puritan as we have been
using the term. He concerned himself neither with the question
of church government nor the related problem of the enforcement
of godliness.

Mede's definition of the true church with all its
conservative implications as to the desirable degree of
reformation was no doubt one of the reasons why his
contemporaries found it easy to accept his opinions on the
millennium. His conception of the thousand-year reign of the
saints, which he thought might begin soon, did not carry with it
the presumption that further reformation of the church was not
only desirable but inevitable. Furthermore Mede maintained his
opinions with a modesty not normally associated with ardent
millennialists. As his translator put it, "that opinion . . .
concerning the 1000 yeers Raigne of Christ, . . . howsoever it
be not received by many as Orthodox, yet is delivered with that
moderation and subjection to the censure of the Church, that it
can displease no man; nor is it (for ought I can see) contrary
to the Analogie of Faith; and may bee usefull for the conversion
of the Iewes."[62] If Mede's opinions were delivered "with such
modestie and moderation that . . . the Printing of [them] will
not be perillous,"[63] there were, as we shall see, men who were
willing to combine them with more puritanical ideas on the
nature of the true church and use this combination as a basis
for agitation for more far-reaching reforms.

---

[62]Joseph Mede, The Key of the Revelation, trans. Richard
More (London, 1643), "The Translator to the Reader."

[63]Ibid., "Commons House," signed by Arthur Jackson.

Chapter III.

THE NEW ENGLAND WAY

The times required reformation. At the end of Queen
Elizabeth's reign a Protestant England had conceded this.
Antichrist had to be repudiated; the man of sin had to be struck
down once and for all. The fruition of God's plan for the
redemption of His elect demanded it. But what was antichristian
and what was not? Men searched the Word of God and striving to
recreate a primitive purity created controversy. Nearly all
were agreed that a sufficient reformation of doctrine had been
achieved by the Elizabethan settlement. The controversy was
over other matters, specifically the ordinances of worship and
church government. Did the Scriptures justify the wearing of
vestments, the use of set prayers in God's worship? Who was to
exercise the power of church discipline, particularly the
ordinance of excommunication--the pasters of each congregation
or the bishops? And what was the proper relationship between
church and state? Should those who governed the church be
granted civil authority too as were the bishops?

Some insisted that all these problems had been rightly
solved at the beginning of good Queen Bess's reign. The
established Anglican Church did not conserve antichristian
corruptions but godly traditions sanctified by age-old usage.
But other men, Puritans, were convinced that a more complete
reformation was necessary. In particular they demanded a purer
discipline in the churches, one under the control of godly
ministers who would be denied magisterial powers and thus freed
from the temptations of politics. As all men knew, the
degeneracy of the Church of Rome had come about because the Pope
had greedily engrossed great temporal as well as spiritual
power. Christians must be wary of believing that "this honour
is given vnto vs, either to trouble the ciuile State, or els to
intermingle Church-governement with civile."[1] Still other
men, Separatists, insisted that only a total departure from the
institutions of Antichrist would suffice to fulfill the
requirements of the times. The visible church should properly
be constituted of believers only, men prepared to acknowledge
the regiment of Christ by voluntarily placing themselves under
the discipline of His church. Only congregations thus created

---

[1]Brightman, 19.

could be sure of having left the ways of the Beast completely
behind. Another group, perhaps even fewer in number than the
Separatists, felt that this kind of congregational reform could
and should take place within the Church of England. This they
believed was necessary to preserve the continuity of the church
throughout history.

All of these different opinions on the amount of reformation
required by the exigencies of the times did agree in one
respect, namely, that the most strenous of efforts to purify the
church necessarily had to be limited to externals. Worship
could be pared to the bare bones of sermons and sacraments;
censures and admonitions could be used to exclude the obviously
profane and profligate from communion; churches could be
covenanted out of godly professors. But in every case it was
beyond the power of men to create a church that was as pure in
substance as it was in form. No church on earth could require
its members to be absolutely regenerate. God alone knew the
constituency of His elect. Until the second coming of the Son
of Man, the earthly church and the heavenly church would never
be identical.

In time one of these groups--by far the most conservative
--gained ascendency in the English church and began to entrench
the kind of reform that stretched only as far as doctrine. With
a king on the throne whose sympathies were anything but Puritan,
the hope for further reformation seemed dim indeed. A handful
of Puritans, those who believed the Church of England should be
purified from within along congregational lines, decided to try
their method in America. There, to the consternation of their
colleagues at home they came to the conclusion that a virtually
pure church could be created in this world simply by excluding
all but the visibly regenerate from membership. Assuming as a
calculated risk that a certain number of hypocrites would slip
through their rigid screening process, they were still prepared
to maintain that they could discern the workings of grace or the
lack thereof within the hearts of other men. In Massachusetts
the invisible church was about to solidify before the skeptical
eyes of the world.

The obvious question, of course, is why they suddenly became convinced that a visibly regenerate church membership was both necessary and possible in the campaign against Antichrist. There was no precedent for their decision in English reform. When they first arrived, they were apparently committed at most to no more than churches composed to professing believers, men and women whose godly conversation and affirmation of a "historical faith" distinguished them from obviously profane and obstinate sinners. During the first few years of the colony's existence, church membership required no confession of saving grace. The people who came to Massachusetts were highly familiar with the process by which a man acquired such grace. Their ministers in England had been educating them in the mysterious operations of the Spirit upon human minds and hearts for at least a generation. By 1630 the answer to that burning question of the Reformation, "How can I know whether I am saved?" had been scaled down to a last, irreducible nubbin of uncertainty by Puritan preachers. But while the New England Way was inconceivable without such knowledge, by itself, it was no warrant for insisting upon a regenerate church membership. Nobody in England up to this time--for all their preoccupation with the process of regeneration--had felt called upon to advocate such a step.

In New England the innovation seems to have been introduced by John Cotton, a highly respected leader of congregationalist reform in the old country. Cotton, who had been associated with the Massachusetts venture from its inception, did not actually arrive in the colony until 1633, whereupon the newly founded churches--apparently under the influence of his preaching--soon began to require evidence of regeneration before admitting new members. The most interesting thing about Cotton's innovation is that only three years before, he had held an entirely different view of church membership. In 1630 he certainly would not have denied admittance to people whose only qualifications were an understanding of church doctrine and a good conversation.[2] Sometime between 1630 and 1633 Cotton had come to the conclusion that saving faith, which he considered the essence of the invisible church, should also be made the essential ingredient of the earthly church.

---

[2] Edmund S. Morgan, _Visible Saints: The History of a Puritan Idea_ (New York, 1963), 64-112.

Cotton's reasons for changing his mind will probably never be known. He himself attributed the change to a further study of the Scriptures--which passages he did not specify--that convinced him participation in the covenant of grace was the sine qua non of church membership. "The Covenant of Grace doth make a People, a joyned People with God, and therefore a church of God."[3] The aspiration toward purity in a man or in a nation was genuine only if it sprang from a principle of grace. Mere rigidity in externals was not a manifestation of grace but of a false and legal righteousness. "When men have received ease from God, and then are streight laced towards their Brethren, then doth the Lord revoke his Pardon. So that Reformation is no assurance that God hath made an everlasting Covenant with us. And mind you further, All the Graces that you have laid hold upon, have sprung from your own Righteousness."[4] If men in this reforming age wished to remake the church on earth, they must perforce begin with the pure in heart, the visible saints. It might well be that the next step in the divine plan to defeat Antichrist would be just such a manifestation of Christ's Kingdom in visibly regenerate churches. If reformation proceeded by degrees from one age to the next toward ultimate consummation and if this were truly the last age--as the existence of Antichrist implied--then it stood to reason that the purification of forms already achieved should logically be followed by a purification of the substance of the church.

Whether or not Cotton actually reasoned in this way during the three years before he came to America, we shall probably never know. There is evidence that by 1639 he was specifically associating the idea of a visibly regenerate church with the second coming. In that year he preached a long series of sermons expounding Revelation, some of which were taken down in shorthand and eventually published in London. The series, however, is not complete. Before we examine Cotton's writings in greater detail, therefore, it might be useful to look at an exposition on Revelation written by another important advocate

---

[3]John Cotton, A Sermon Preached . . . at Salem, 1636 (Boston, 1713), 21.

[4]Ibid., 31.

of the New England Way, Thomas Goodwin. Goodwin was a Puritan
clergyman who became a leader of congregational reform, or
Independency as it was called, during the Civil Wars and the
Interregnum. Outside of America he was probably the foremost
theologian of the New England Way. His analysis of the
Apocalypse, which like Cotton's was written in 1639, is of
particular interest for our problem since he was converted to
Independency by Cotton in 1633--just before the latter sailed to
New England.

In Goodwin's eyes the Book of Revelation was a coherent,
logical, and tightly constructed piece of work, comparable to a
well written play. God, revealing the story of His Kingdom
within history, had done so as skillfully as the greatest
playwright. In St. John's vision just as in ordinary plays the
stage was set, a chorus provided to give judgment and
approbation ("the custom in comedies of old"), and a prologue
read. The history of the Kingdom thus began with a description
of the church, the stage upon which the true meaning of man's
sojourn on earth would become apparent. The chorus was provided
by its members, who throughout the ages "upon any great or
solemn occasion [gave] their _plaudite_ or acclamation of glory
unto God."[5] All of this was represented to St. John in the
vision of the throne, the four beasts, and the twenty-four
elders described in the fourth chapter of Revelation. Like his
predecessors, Goodwin too regarded this chapter as depicting the
church _sub species aeternitatis_. It was "a representation of
the church (wherein God hath his throne) of men on earth,
universal in all ages; set forth according to the form or
pattern of institution of a church, into which all saints on
earth should be moulded."[6] Naturally this universal pattern
was a simple one. In the ideal church there were but two
components--the congregation and its officers. The elders
represented the brethren who held "the radical power," while the
four beasts were the officers who, "though nearest the throne,
yet are mentioned after the elders; for though their place be

---

[5]Goodwin, III, 1.

[6]_Ibid._, 2.

nearer, yet they are but the church's servants."[7] Once the
stage was set, the prologue showed how Christ had taken upon
Himself the work of the redemption of the elect, having the
power and providence not only to know but to execute the decrees
of God for all time. Finally, after the prologue had been read,
"God's design and project upon the world" began to unfold, and
the drama of the church in the world--from Christ's ascension to
His return--was played out for the edification of all ages.

Goodwin saw the church's story in much the same way that his
predecessors had seen it. Essentially it was a tale of gradual
decline from primitive godliness to the depths of Antichristian
corruption and equally gradual ascent into the light of the
Reformation. Above all, it was a description of the execution
of Christ's government in history, "first, in putting down all
opposite rule and power that stand in his way, . . . and,
secondly, in a visible taking the kingdom to himself and his
saints, which makes the fifth monarchy."[8] The rough outline
of the story went like this. Upon His ascension to heaven,
Christ had found the Roman empire--the fourth monarchy--spread
throughout the world. Everywhere He was to seat His Kingdom and
church, He found the dominion of Satan. Hence He began the
conquest of the world by preaching the gospel and within three
hundred years had subjected the empire to Himself by converting
it and its rulers to Christianity. But in revenge for previous
persecutions against His saints, Christ brought down Rome's
imperial power and divided the empire into two parts by means of
the wars of the Goths in the west and those of the Saracens in
the east. The western empire was divided again into ten
kingdoms, all of which consented to give their power to the
Pope, who thus restored the Roman monarchy to its full glory.
In both east and west during the period of dissolution, Christ
had sealed up 144,000 saints--men who had opposed, however
unsuccessfully, the rising tide of corruption and degeneracy.

---

[7]Ibid., 4.

[8]Ibid., 27.

But now with the Pope on one hand and the Turk on the other,
"Christ [had] a new business of it yet, to come unto his
kingdom, and as difficult as ever."[9] Therefore He brought
forth seven vials containing the seven last plagues to dispatch
the Pope and the Turk and wholly root them out. With the
appearance of these vials, the world entered into its last
age--the time in which Christ would bring His earthly Kingdom to
perfection through the total destruction of His enemies. Here
the Apocalypse told the story of the church "both in respect of
the progress of its separation further and further off from
Rome, and so of its increase of light, purity, and reformation;
as likewise in respect of persecutions and judgments upon it,
and its restitution and deliverance again from under them."[10]

The first vial had been poured out upon Antichrist by the
Waldensians, who about the year 100 had erected true churches
and preached a doctrine of both law and gospel. Their
persecution and consequent dispersal throughout Europe had been
the means of furthering the spread of truth and light. From
their descendants, Wyclif, Huss, and Jerome of Prague had
learned that the Pope was Antichrist and had been inspired to
advocate reforms in the church. Their work had marked the
pouring out of the second vial. The third one was embodied in
the preaching of Luther. He had shown beyond a doubt that
separation from Rome was mandatory for God's saints and had thus
prepared the way for the fourth vial which was the present
period of "glorious peace and sunshine of the gospel." After
the grievous persecutions of earlier ages, the church was now
enjoying a time of harvest during which the elect were being
converted and gathered in by the preaching of the gospel. Most
important of all, "this preaching of the gospel, that hath
reaped this corn, hath been authorized by the chief magistrates,
and by kingly power, even whole kingdoms professing. . .Jesus

---

[9]Ibid., 28.

[10]Ibid., 80.

Christ, the Son of man, is visibly set in the throne, ruling by
Christian magistrates, they using their power for him."[11]
After harvest comes vintage, and the vintage which even now was
following the harvest of the elect was one of vengeance. God
was cutting down the wild grapes in His vineyard and casting
them into the wine-press of His wrath.

> And these grapes are those carnal Protestants and professors
> of religion, who together with the elect, have enjoyed the
> heat of this fair long summer, and hung like to grapes in
> the sun, but retaining their sourness, have been ripened
> indeed, but only for wrath and vengeance. And lo, how this
> sharp sickle hath gone up and down in Germany for well-nigh
> these twenty years, being such a wine-press of fierce wrath,
> and such a treading down to an overflowing of blood and
> misery, as hath scarce been paralleled in any age! For it
> is the vengeance of the temple, not so much destroyed, as
> defiled and dishonoured by their mixture; which as much
> provokes God unto wrath as the persecution of his temple
> would have done.[12]

All of this--both harvest and vintage--was contained within
the fourth vial. There were three yet to go, and these three
would encompass the final destruction of the powers of
darkness. The fifth, which would strike at the seat of Babylon
(i.e., Rome), Goodwin thought was just beginning. It would be
completed about 1666 and would be followed by the destruction of
the Turks (the sixth vial). Then the remnants of the forces of
the Pope and Turk would unite with all the evil kings of the
world and fight against the Christians and the Jews--who would
have been converted in 1650--until "Christ himself comes and
makes but one work of it, with his own hand from heaven
destroying them."[13] This victory would initiate the
millennial reign of Christ, and Goodwin predicted that it would
take place in 1700.

---

[11] Ibid., 89.

[12] Ibid.

[13] Ibid., 28.

This was the outline of the story of the church from
Christ's ascension to the end of time. The part of it which
most interested Goodwin was the part that applied to his own
age. "The main thing I aimed at, both in my first studying this
book, and also in this my exposition of it, was to search into
such passages therein as did concern and fall upon the last
days, especially the present times of the church; and to inquire
and find out under which of these constellations our own times
do fall, and what is certainly yet to come."[14] To the end
that he might properly present his findings concerning the last
days, Goodwin devoted over half of his book to a detailed
analysis of the period from "the Church's separation from
Popery" to the appearance of New Jerusalem. The whole of this
period Goodwin divided into three "reformations," each
corresponding to certain vials and each described in a separate
chapter of Revelation. The first of these was the "separation
of the church from Antichrist in several degrees"--the
reformation of doctrine and worship already accomplished by the
first reformers. It corresponded to the first four vials and
brought the church up to Goodwin's time. The second reformation
was just beginning with the end of the fourth and the start of
the fifth vials. It was to be a purification of the membership
of the church. Finally, the last reformation--which would bring
history to a close--was to be a "reformation personal, of the
saints themselves in it, as then with might and main preparing
and adorning themselves for the marriage of the Lamb, which then
they shall evidently see approaching, now when the whore is cast
off and burnt; and there you may see them getting all the fine
linen they can,--that is, of holiness and growth in grace, 'the
righteousness of the saints.'"[15]

---

[14]Ibid., 78.

[15]Ibid., 82.

Before this glorious third reformation could be consummated, however, the membership of the church had to be purified from its present "profane mixture." The second reformation was the work <u>now</u> required of the saints in God's plan for the church, and Goodwin took care to expound the chapter in which it was described--Chapter 11--at length. This chapter more than any other in Revelation Goodwin felt exactly represented "the present face, the affairs, stirrings, and alterations now a-working in the churches of Europe."[16] In this part of his vision, St. John is commanded by an angel to measure the temple, the altar, and the worshippers which appear before him, expressly omitting the outer court of the Gentiles. Goodwin interpreted this act as a representation of the "face of the church" in the age "wherein Antichrist's reign is drawing near to its end"--"(this age, as I take it)."[17] The temple was the church and St. John's measurement of it the reformation that would make it "more answerable to the pattern in the mount." Omitting to measure the outer court meant that the church was to be purified of its profane mixture of carnal and unregenerate professors. Even though true churches had already been set up during the first reformation--by virtue of the elect hidden within them--they were yet defiled by the presence of this outer court "into which all sorts came." They were, therefore, more outward courts than inward temples. Their promiscuous mixture of regenerate men with carnal professors permitted great corruptions both in church fellowship and in church worship. Hence it was the duty of the saints to carry reformation one step further by purging the visible church of its unregenerate members.

> And observe the glorious wisdom that is in God's proceeding herein, as the reason of it. For God intending to have a church most holy unto himself, under the seventh trumpet, in which 'the ark shall be seen,'. . . and his manner being to carry on his church unto perfection by degrees,--he doth therefore, about the midst of that time, between the first

---

[16] <u>Ibid.</u>, 124.

[17] <u>Ibid.</u>, 122.

reformation long since made and that seventh trumpet, in an
age or so foregoing it, set his builders on work (whom John
here represents) to endeavour to erect a new frame, and a
reformation of that reformation; and to take the reed, and
measure over anew both temple, altar, and worshippers, and
to cast out that outward court of worshippers, with those
corruptions of theirs which hindered that thorough
reformation; and so to contract his temple into a narrower
compass, as the proportion of the inner temple to the
outward was, yet purer and more refined, he delighting more
in truth, and purity of worship, than in magnitude or
multitude of sacrificers and worshippers: and so to make to
himself a church that shall consist of priests, and an
inward temple separated from that outward court, into which
the true worshippers are called up from the other, which
before lay common to both.[18]

Goodwin was careful to point out that by the inner temple he did
not mean the invisible communion of God's elect which existed
apart from any visible church. The imagery of the inner temple
and the outer court was not a type of the old distinction
between the visible and invisible churches. The temple
represented "churches or congregations of public worshippers
considered as such; church-fellowship, as you call it."[19] The
altar represented the ordinances of worship, and the worshippers
were the saints. The act of measuring was simply:

By the word exactly putting a difference between them that
fear God and them that fear him not; measuring out who fear
him by marks, signs, and spots upon his people, (as in
Deuteronomy God speaks,) which the word gives. And this
distinguishing and putting a difference between men and men,
the word calls excluding or leaving them out. Which,
accordingly, to make way for the right constitution of
churches, in discerning the true matter of them, hath been

---

[18]Ibid., 128.

[19]Ibid., 129.

the chief work of the godly ministers in England in this
last age; who, though they wanted the ordinance of
excommunication in their churches, yet in lieu of it they
had excommunicating gifts, and were forced, because of that
profane mixture in churches, to spend most of their ministry
in distinguishing men, by giving signs and marks of men's
natural and regenerate estates, and convincing and
discovering carnal men to themselves and others: which God
in providence ordained, to make way for the erection of more
pure churches. For by this light was set up in godly men's
hearts a spirit to discern between the clean and the
unclean; and so to hew and set apart the materials for this
temple, as the stones for Solomon's were.[20]

In spite of his emphasis on the necessity of constructing
churches out of pure (i.e., regenerate) members, Goodwin did not
believe the church would become absolutely pure before the
advent of the New Jerusalem. Until that time there would always
be hypocrites in the church--despite the most stringent
requirements for admissions. "For though their second
reformation, and the reed thereof, keeps out men civil and
profane, whom John here represents, may judge visibly so to be;
yet many a hypocrite, that maketh a like, may scape and crowd
into this inward temple still, whilst the judgment of men, who
often err, applies this reed. But into the other temple to
come, under the new Jerusalem, shall none of these enter."[21]
In the meantime a church that denied entrance to the
unregenerate to the best of its knowledge would be the most
adequate means of protecting the saints from the degeneracy
which was an inevitable concomitant of the world's old age. "To
get into this temple is the greatest preservative to keep the
saints from the over-growing corruptions and defilements of
these Gentiles [i.e., carnal Protestants]; and it may unto many
prove a protection and sanctuary from their power, as to those

---

[20] Ibid., 130-31.

[21] Ibid., 128.

churches in New England it may be hoped it shall. 'God will create a defense upon his glory.' And, however, they shall hereby be reserved for that resurrection which afterward is to come."[22]

Goodwin did not doubt that this second reformation would take place in the midst of degeneracy and corruption. It seemed likely that its raison d'etre was to line up those who could be trusted in the coming fight against the forces of Satan. In Goodwin's judgment--being "not swayed unto it through affection only"--the purest professors were to be found in his own land. England, therefore, must hasten to prepare for its leading role in the coming struggle by erecting the kind of churches the New Englanders already had founded. Only in this manner could the challenge of these perilous times be met. On this note, Goodwin ended his exposition of the Apocalypse:

> But, however, let an indefinite warning that these things are approaching, and we within reach of them, suffice for to move us to prepare for them, which is the only use of knowing them. . . . [For] we are to consider that we live now in the extremity of times, when motions and alterations, being so near the centre, become quickest and speediest; and we are at the verge, and, as it were, within the whirl of that great mystery of Christ's kingdom, which will, as a gulf, swallow up all time; and so, the nearer we are unto it, the greater and more sudden changes will Christ make, now hastening to make a full end of all.[23]

If Goodwin believed that England should prepare for a leading role in the tumultuous days ahead, John Cotton was willing to give his native land more than a little credit for reformation already accomplished. In one of the three published parts of his sermons on the Apocalypse, The Powring Out of the Seven Vials, he assigned England a major role in bringing about the reforms which any day now would complete the destruction of Antichrist. These reforms he thought were the antitypes of the seven vials described in Revelation--just as Goodwin did. Unlike Goodwin though, he did not think that the vials could be

---

[22]Ibid., 130.

[23]Ibid., 204.

correlated with the appearance of the Waldensians five centuries ago.[24] Instead Cotton believed the first vial had been pouredout as recently as the reigns of Henry, Edward, and Mary when English martyrs had announced the theme of reformation. These men and women had been "such as did convince [men] of the Damnable estate of a Catholike, and taught them, that by their Religion they could go not beyond a Reprobate; . . . that all their Religion was but the worship of God after the devises of men, even Will-worship, such as they were led into by the Man of Sinne."[25] Their work was reinforced soon after by "Chenmitius, and Junius, Chamier, Whitaker, and Reignolds, Perkins, and Ames, and the rest of the holy Saints of God, that have poured out this [second] viall of Gods wrath, that is, that by their doctrine and writings from the word have poured out such cleare conviction, and refutation of [Catholic] doctrine and worship."[26] Just as corruption had crept into the church by degrees, the vials of God's wrath were progressively discovering the "pollution in Religion."

---

[24]Cotton did, however, believe that reformation had begun with the Waldensians and had continued and spread throughout Europe until it had openly broken forth with Luther. He merely did not think these events should be correlated with the seven vials. See his An Exposition upon the Thirteenth Chapter of Revelation.

[25]John Cotton, The Powring Out of the Seven Vials (London, 1642), "The First Viall," 4-5.

[26]Ibid., "The Second Viall," 20. The men referred to by Cotton are Martin Chemnitz (1522-1586), German theologian known for his work against the Council of Trent; Franciscus Junius (1545-1602), French Reformed theologian who wrote against Bellarmine; Daniel Chamier (1565-1621), French Reformed preacher who presided over the synod which added an article to the Reformed confession of faith declaring the Pope to be Antichrist; William Whitaker (1548-1595), English theologian who wrote against Bellarmine; John Reynolds (1549-1607), Puritan divine, author of several works against Catholics; William Perkins (1558-1602), English theologian greatly revered by New England Puritans; William Ames (1576-1633), another English theologian who profoundly influenced New England Puritanism.

Queen Elizabeth with the aid of Parliament had been responsible for the third vial. This one, which turned rivers and fountains to blood, had been "effectually accomplished" when a law was passed in 1581 requiring that any Jesuits or Catholic priests found within the realm be judged guilty of high treason. In this manner, the "rivers and fountains" of Catholic propaganda had--quite literally--been turned into blood.[27] The angel who declared the righteousness of the Lord in visiting this plague upon Catholicism Cotton thought was none other than William Cecil. His book, Justitia Britanniae, had made it clear that what had been decreed in Parliament was just according to the Law of God and the true principles of "the Christian State Policie." The Netherlands had followed England's example in 1586. Together these laws had "raised all Christendome in combustion, the wars of eighty eight, the Spanish invasion had speciall respect to this, and had not the Lord borne witnesse to his people and their Law, in defeating the intendments of their enemies, against both the Nations, it might have been the ruine of them both."[28]

Cotton gave his listeners a choice when it came to the fourth vial. It could be taken either as the defeat of Austria by Sweden, or the breaking of the Pope's civil supremacy by Queen Elizabeth when she defied his bull of excommunication. Since then, as everyone knew, his power had greatly decreased--even in Catholic nations. The fifth vial, which was supposed to be poured out upon the seat of the Beast, Cotton did not interpret as a visitation threatened against Rome. Rather, since the seat of the Beast really existed in the papal and episcopal forms of church government, this prediction would be fulfilled in an attack upon these corruptions. Indeed, the first drops of this vial had already been sprinkled by Beza, Cartwright, Baynes, and Parker and even now the rest of it was descending full force in Scotland.

---

[27]See the account of the executions of three Catholic priests which took place in Cotton's home town when he was a young boy in Larzer Ziff, The Career of John Cotton: Puritanism and the American Experience (Princeton, J.J., 1962), 3-4.

[28]Cotton, The Powring Out of the Seven Vials, "The Third Vial," 7.

> You now see whole Vialls full of wrath powred out by the
> whole Church of Scotland, who have engaged themselves, and
> their state for ever in this quarrell, and have beene
> carried along herein, not in a way of popular tumult, but
> with such wisedome, courage, judgment and Piety, that you
> may see and say that it is not a Viall powred out by an
> unadvised multitude, but by an Angell of God, by the
> Heavenly Ministers of his wrath.[29]

From Scotland the wrath of God against these degenerate church
governments was pouring into England. Men questioned the
episcopacy--let alone the papacy--as they never had before.
Cotton believed this growing doubt would spread from Great
Britain through the Catholic countries to the very gates of Rome
itself.

The fifth vial would be followed very shortly by the sixth,
which was to dry up the river Euphrates. Cotton conceived this
river to be the idolatry and revenues which nourished both the
Pope and the Turk. The ten Christian kings of Europe, converted
under the fifth vial (Cotton did not identify them), would "dry
up all these [papal] revenewes." This would deprive the Turks
by encouraging the conversion of the Jews, who would invade the
East and thus cut off the maintenance of the Turkish rulers.
The sixth vial was not to affect Europe alone. Its appearance--
which in some degree had already begun--had implications for New
England as well, since the drying up of idolatry referred not
only to graven images but to the idols Mammon erected in the
hearts of all men:

> And so will God deale with our Cattell if they be our Gods,
> they shall either be worth little, or else he will deny us
> fodder for them; if they devoure our spirits, and take off
> our mindes from the Ordinances of God; he will rend away
> anything that standeth between him and our soules;
> Therefore, as ever we desire that we may prosper, and that
> their [sic] may be a ready way prepared for our comfort, let
> no streames of Idolatry, be found among us, . . .Only let us
> take part with this Angell in powring out Vialls upon the

---

[29]Ibid., "The Fift Vial," 4.

corruptions that are found in our own hearts; look that
their be no corruptions in us, but such as are stil drying
and drying up, and see if God be not faithfull and gratious
to us aboundantly; stir we up our selves therefore, and one
another hereunto, then shall we see Gods ancient people [the
Jews] brought home and the Lord shall be one over al the
Earth, and his name one, which wil prove a Resurrection unto
all the Churches of the Saints.[30]

If New Englanders would turn from the pursuit of earthly
goods to the cultivation of greater righteousness, they would be
rewarded with the blessed spectacle of the conversion of the
Jews and the reign of Christ through the world--nothing less
that the beginning of the millennium. Cotton like Goodwin
thought that Christ, "by his Spirit and in his Servants," would
reign a thousand years on earth and that His reign would begin
just as soon as the power of the Word, breaking forth throughout
the world in the seventh vial, had finally defeated Antichrist.
Whether or not New England dried up its own streams of idolatry,
Cotton thought all of this would probably happen very soon. "I
know not what you that are young may live unto, for the neerer
these things come unto their accomplishment, the swifter their
motion will be, as it is with all naturall motions."[31] The
question for New England was whether it would be rewarded or
punished by the millennium.

Cotton put these alternatives to his colonial listeners in
blunt terms in his sermons on the verses in Revelation which
speak of the first resurrection.[32] The first resurrection,
which would be spiritual, not bodily, would take place about the
time of Antichrist's fall and would consist of two parts--the
first being the resurrection of particular persons "restored and
renewed by regenerating Grace" and the second being a
resurrection of the churches "when as they are recovered againe

[30]Ibid., "The Sixth Viall," 26.

[31]Ibid., "The Fourth Part vpon the Sixt Viall," 11.

[32]Rev. 20: 5,6.

from their Apostatical and dead estate in Idolatry and
Superstition."[33] The two parts were interdependent:

> The particular members of the church rise by regeneration
> and the work of Gods grace in their hearts working in them
> by his spirit all grace to salvation: Faith, Hope, Patience,
> Humility, etc. Now they rising againe, not into a loose
> frame, but a state rising into a Church body, and the Church
> body so reformed as may beare witnesse against all
> Antichristianisme in doctrine, Worship and government; This
> is the first resurrection.[34]

Cotton was careful to emphasize that the particular members
making up these reformed churches would be "sincere members,"
for otherwise "it could not bee said those men are blessed and
holy that have part in the first resurrection, if they had part
only in outward reformation."[35] Such reformed churches would
truly constitute a "sincere and spirituall community."

The first part of this resurrection-reformation, the
conversion of particular members, had clearly already begun, but
the second part would be fully accomplished only upon the
ruination of Antichrist. "I cannot speake according to my Text,
and say there is the first resurrection of Churches yet: Though
there be a resurrection of Christians, and a yawning towards
further reformation' in these Churches."[36] When Antichrist
did fall, though, there would be "a fresh supply of a notable
reformation, and notable judgements upon wicked men."[37]
Nations all over the world would then be blessed with the
opportunity to reform. The "beauty of the Ordinances" the
allure of "so many Sincere hearted Christians in the Church"

---

[33] John Cotton, The Churches Resurrection (London, 1642),
8.

[34] Ibid., 9.

[35] Ibid., 10.

[36] Ibid., 19.

[37] Ibid., 12.

would bring multitudes into the fold. For those who did not
succumb to the attractions of godliness at that time, however,
there would be a terrible punishment. They and their posterity
would be given no opportunity to partake of reformation during
all the years when Christ's servants would rule the earth.
"Such Nations and people as are not renewed and restored in the
first resurrection, upon the destruction of Antichrist and the
ruine of Rome, they shall not recover the like liberty, either
of Reformation of themselves, or of persecution of the Churches
for a thousand yeeres after."[38] The moral for New England was
obvious:

> The use of this point is First a serious and strong warning
> unto all the people of God that shall live when Antichrist
> shall be abolished, and Rome ruinated: Take heed how you
> slip such opportunities of turning unto God: If men grow
> not more sincere and pure in seeking after God (whether they
> be publick States or private persons:) If men be not
> brought on, but will stand out such glorious reformation
> then, and such powerfull providences then; If men stand out
> then, and not bee awakened, it is to bee feared they will
> not be awakened, (nor men of their Spirits) for a thousand
> yeares together.[39]

God might yet bear with New England for a while, but if the
colonists did not now "strike a fast Covenant with our God to be
his people," then they would be cast into outer darkness when
Christ's Kingdom was established on earth. Surely this was the
time to remember that "we are not like to see greater
incouragements for a good while then now we see."[40]

However much Cotton was prepared to question the "sincerity"
of New England's reformation, he was still convinced that it was
moving in the right direction. His description of the
millennium, which he thought might begin as soon as 1655, sounds
very like the holy commonwealth already established in
Massachusetts.

---

[38]_Ibid._, 11-12.

[39]_Ibid._, 14-15.

[40]_Ibid._, 16.

These thousand yeares therefore doe most properly begin from
the throwing down of Antichrist and destruction of Rome; The
Lord will then send such powerfull Ministers into the
Church, that by the power of the keyes they shall take hold
on Satan that is to say, convince him and his instruments of
all Popish, and Paganish Religion and binde him by the
Chaine, that is to say, the strong chaine of Gods
Ordinances, Word and Sacraments, and Censures:

They shall not take hold of Satan in his own Person, for I
doe believe Satan will ever be at liberty to tempt the
Sonnes of men; and he is never so cast into the bottomlesse
pit, but he hath a power to vexe the Sonnes of men to the
end of the world: But he speakes of Satan in his
instruments, that not one of them shall appeare, but the
Lord in his Word shall take hold on them and abandon them;
and if they be Church members will bind them in chaines of
the Ordinances of God, as Admonition, and Excommunication
and hold them so close to it, that such wickednesse shall
not abide uncontrouled on the face of the Earth chiefly by
Church Censures, and partly also by punishment from Civil
Magistrates as need shall be.[41]

Men would then "clearely know that the true Church is not a
Catholike visible, nor a Cathedrall, nor a Diocesan, nor a
Provinciall Church."[42] They would realize that true churches
were particular congregations made up of visible saints,
exercising discipline according to God's ordinances, and they
would establish such churches throughout the world. When this
was accomplished, the millennium would have arrived. Then it
could truly be said, "It is done; Even all that God hath to do
in the world, for any further Reformation expect it not."[43]

---

[41] Ibid., 5-6.

[42] Cotton, The Powring Out of the Seven Vials, "The Seventh
Vial," 11.

[43] Ibid.

By now the similarities between Goodwin's and Cotton's interpretations of the Apocalypse should be evident. Both believed that the fall of Antichrist would probably take place within the lifetime of people then living, that this fall would be accompanied by a reformation of churches similar to that practised in New England, that this reformation would initiate the millennium, and that even now the way for all this was being prepared by the restoration of excommunication or "excommunicating gifts," which served to separate the visibly regenerate from the visibly profane. Neither man could be called a pre-millennialist since both expected this great reformation to develop out of a historical process that had already been in progress for several centuries. Nor were they prepared to claim absolute accuracy in the discernment of hypocrites short of Judgment Day. Satan--who was, of course, not identical with Antichrist--would merely be bound by the ordinances of God during the millennium, not destroyed. What Goodwin and Cotton envisaged was a great period within history during which it would be given to the saints to restrain evil through the righteous exercise of civil and ecclesiastical authority. It would be a thousand-year extension of the New England Way. This did not imply that the Saints could bring the millennium on unaided. Even the beginnings that were being made in New England depended upon a divine covenant, and there was still a danger that the experiment might fail through the carelessness of the experimenters. Goodwin and Cotton did not expect to establish the millennium through the action of the saints. The rule of the saints would become inevitable because a growing knowledge of the Lord would transform the hearts of men. As Cotton put it:

And when once the light of the Gospell is dispersed, it will bring in all Nations, it will thunder upon them, and never leave untill it have changed them. If this knowledge of God come amongst an army of men, they will not touch any thing that is their brethrens, not meddle, not make with any to doe them harme, no mans purse shall be taken from him, no mans goods taken away without due recompence, only they will not be deluded with shaddowes, nor suffer mountaines to overtop them, neither will they be encompassed with hands: they will raise such an earthquake first, in Church, and Common-wealth, as you will at length wonder at, for though

it begin in a corner of the world, it will not cease till it
have shaken all Christendome, for when men once begin
clearly to see which is the true Church of God, that it is
not Cathedrall, nor Provinciall, nor Diocesan, but
congregationall only, the officers whereof are godly
Pastors, and Teachers, and ruling Elders, and Deacons. And
when they see that the Saints which they have embraced, and
esteemed, are not the true Saints of God, nor these the
Churches, nor those the officers of Christ wherewith they
have been gulled: but they see now who are the Saints of the
most high; and can put a difference now between precious and
vile: In this way men will goe on to raise such an
earthquake (and that not besides the Law neither) that if
any City rise up against them, fall it must and stoop unto
them, and at length Rome it self shall fall, and all the
Cities of the Nations that cleave unto her, and every
mountaine shall bee rooted up, and all their consecrated
places shall lie levell with the common soile, this will the
Lord bring to passe, and will not leave till he hath wrought
his great work in the world.[44]

There were other ministers in New England beside John Cotton
who thought along apocalyptic lines. Perhaps the one whose
views were closest to those of Cotton was John Davenport, the
first minister of New Haven. Davenport, like his close friend
Thomas Goodwin, was converted to the cause of congregationalism
by Cotton in 1633, just before the latter sailed for New
England. Incurring the displeasure of the bishops shortly
thereafter, Davenport fled to Holland where he became involved
in an acrimonious controversy over baptism and soon returned to
England. Cotton meanwhile had been encouraging him to come to
America by sending him reports--if we can take Cotton Mather's
word for it--"that the order of the churches and the
commonwealth was now so settled in New England, by common
consent, that it brought into his mind the new heaven and the
new earth, wherein dwells righteousness."[45] (Possibly to the
embarrassment of his mentor, Davenport arrived in Massachusetts
just in time to help settle the Antinomian Controversy.) By

---

[44]Ibid., 15-16.

[45]John Cotton, quoted in Cotton Mather, Magnalia Christi
Americana (Hartford, 1855), I, 325.

1638 he was safely established in New Haven. There he set out
to create a church of even greater righteousness than those of
Massachusetts. If the Bay Colony brought to mind the new heaven
and earth, New Haven was intended to exemplify the quintessence
of purity. As Cotton Mather later put it, Davenport's
objectivewas to do "all that was possible to render the renowned
church of New-Haven like the New-Jerusalem."[46]

Davenport's desire to model the church of New Haven upon the
New Jerusalem is especially interesting in the light of his
views upon the millennium. Like Goodwin and Cotton, he too
believed there would be an extended period on earth in which the
church would enjoy as much "perfection of light, and holiness,
and love, as is attainable on this side of heaven."[47] Unlike
them, however, Davenport was a chiliast who believed Christ
would reign on earth personally during the millennium, although
he did not believe the saints would enjoy carnal pleasures at
this time. These views, as he well knew, were dangerously close
to those held by such millennial enthusiasts as the
Fifth-Monarchy men. Yet writing in 1667--seven years after the
rule of saints in England had utterly collapsed--Davenport
refused to renounce his chiliasm. "Concerning this his second
coming, to set up his Kingdom on earth, some acknowledge no
kingdom of Christ on earth, but spiritual and invisible in the
hearts of the elect. The kingdom of Christ hath indeed been set
up by his effectual operation of the spirit in the Ministry of
the Gospel, from the first publishing of the Gospel, ...But
there is another, a Political Kingdom of Christ to be set up in
the last times."[48] The Fifth-Monarchy men had erred in two
ways: "First, By anticipating the time, which will not be till

---

[46]Ibid., 328.

[47]John Davenport, "An Epistle to the Reader," in Increase
Mather, The Mystery of Israel's Salvation Explained and Applyed
(London, 1669). Unfortunately, this preface is the only extant
writing of Davenport on the millennium. Cotton Mather, however,
states that he "both preached and wrote" on the subject.
Magnalia Christi Americana, I, 331.

[48]Ibid.

the pouring out of the sixth and seventh Vials. Secondly, By putting themselves upon a work which shall not be done by men, but by Christ himself."[49] In spite of his strictures against the Fifth Monarchists for "anticipating the time," Davenport apparently believed the second coming was near for he noted "constant reports from sundry places and hands" that the Israelites were converging upon Jerusalem from all over the world, "carryed on with great signs and wonders by a high and mighty hand of extraordinary providence." This seemed to him to indicate that the Jews were being assembled by God preparatory to their long prophesied conversion. Since Davenport thought they were not to be converted before "Romes ruine" and Christ's appearance to judge Antichrist, it seems likely that he thought the millennium was near. Davenport supported his views by citing Goodwin, Alsted, and Mede--"(who was no Phanatick, as the Prelates themselves will grant),"--all of whom thought the millennium might begin in the seventeenth century.

Although there is no direct evidence for it, Davenport's apocalyptic views probably dated at least from his early days in New Haven. Mede and Alsted were both published before he left for America, and he apparently maintained a correspondence with Thomas Goodwin. Nor in New England could he have failed to keep in contact with his old friend John Cotton. Certainly Davenport's conception of the millennium was close to that of his two colleagues apart from his insistence upon Christ's personal rule. He too was fascinated by the vision of a coming earthly perfection of the church. It may well be that his strictness in the admission of church members was directly linked to this vision.

Davenport's associate at New Haven, William Hooke, was apparently also a chiliast. Hooke, who came to Massachusetts in 1636, was a minister at Taunton until he moved to New Haven in 1644. He remained there twelve years, returning to England in 1656 to become Oliver Cromwell's chaplain. In 1662 he was ejected from his living. From then until his death in 1678, he led the rather precarious existence of a non-conforming minister. All of Hooke's apocalyptic writings date from after

---

[49]Ibid.

the fall of the Protectorate. Thus although he was sure that
"the world is now drawing towards its end,"[50] he was
understandably primarily concerned with reconciling his readers
to a difficult time in the immediate future. His emphasis was
on hope and faith in the face of adversity. Occasionally,
however, he did suggest that in more propitious times he might
have been an outspoken defender of millennialism. For instance,
in a passage reminiscent of John Cotton, he spoke of "a great
effusion of the Spirit of God" to be expected in the last times:

> Hence it followeth, That there will be a very great light of
> Knowledge in this Day, so that there shall not be so much
> need, as now there is, for one to teach another; saying,
> Know the Lord, for they shall all know him from the least to
> the greatest ... This Light of Knowledg shall have a great
> influence into the Hearts and Lives of Men, who shall shine
> eminently in Holiness; . . . Even Carters, Cooks, and
> Kitchin-Maids shall then shine in purity of life, and there
> shall be no more the Canaanite in the House of the Lord of
> Hosts.[51]

In 1664 he wrote to Davenport that "I lissen much after ye
mocions of ye Turke, wreof ye Intelligencer, every weeke, writes
something. For his slaying of ye 3d pt of men (vis:
Antichrians) Rev: 9.18, 19, 20, 21 and ye slaying of ye
witnesses by ye Beast yt ascendeth out of ye bottomles pit Rev:
11. 7 (I say) these are ye two grte things mentioned to be done
under ye 6th Trumpet, wch some are of opinion is drawing on to
its last blast."[52] It seems very likely that Hooke shared
Davenport's views on the millennium and church membership.

---

[50]William Hooke, <u>A Discourse Concerning the Witnesses,
Relating to the Time, Place, and Manner of their Being Slain</u>
(London, 1681), 33.

[51]William Hooke, <u>A Short Discourse of the Nature and
Extent of the Gospel-Day</u> (London, 1673), 145-46.

[52]Letter to John Davenport, 1664 (from MS copy made by G.
Lyon Turner in Beinecke Library, Yale University).

Davenport, Cotton, and presumably Hooke combined strict
views on church membership with anticipation of the imminent
arrival of the millennium. At the other extreme was someone
like Thomas Parker, son of the well-known Robert Parker who had
been an early advocate of Puritan reforms in England. Unlike
his father, who had leaned toward congregationalism, Thomas
inclined toward a presbyterian form of church government. At
the church in Newbury, Massachusetts over which he and his
cousin James Noyes presided, members were admitted according to
a rule, "so large, that the weakest Christians may bee
received."[53] Parker's views on the millennium were as
flexible as the ones he held on church membership. In a book on
the prophecies of Daniel, he set forth two possible systems of
apocalyptic chronology--one putting the end of Antichrist and
the beginning of New Jerusalem at 1650 and the other at 1860.
When it did come, Parker did not expect New Jerusalem to exist
on earth for more than 45 years. "As concerning the opinion of
many Worthyes, affirming, that the reign of the Saints a 1000
yeers, is to be expected in the glory of New Jerusalem at the
end of the yeers of Antichrist; I cannot possibly bring my
judgement to incline unto it."[54] According to Parker, the
expressions of "temporall felicity" which described New
Jerusalem in the Bible were "either to be understood of its
state of inchoation, . . . especially from after the end of the
years of Antichrist through the space of 45 years, . . . or
being applied to its state of heavenly perfection immediately
ensuing, they are to be understood in a mysticall sense."[55]
Parker thus gave an Augustinian interpretation to the
thousand-year period of Satan's binding. As he saw it, it had
begun either in 620 or in 840 and accordingly would end roughly
a millennium later in the Day of Judgment.

---

[53]Thomas Parker, The True Copy of a Letter (London, 1644),
4.

[54]The Visions and Prophecies of Daniel Expounded (London,
1646), 147.

[55]Ibid., 148.

Parker's main concern, however, was with Daniel's seventy weeks and not the millennium. As was usual, he interpreted the seventy weeks as a period of 490 years during which the true church would be gathered out of the "Spiritual Babylon of Antichrist." This work could date either from 1160 (the Waldensians) or 1370 (Wyclif). In either case it was the time when the church would be "restored and edified by the Ordinances of Christ and Word of truth." At its end (either in 1650 or 1860), there would be established "the Kingdom of Saints, wherein they shall dwell in safety, their enemies rooted out in the space of 45 years, Verse 12. and the elect remnant of them coverted, . . . then many shall rise to life, and many to shame. Thus the generall resurrection is compounded with the last plague on Antichrist."[56] Quite clearly Parker did not go along with Cotton and Davenport when it came to the millennial rule of the saints. Whether this was related to his more lenient views on church membership, it is impossible to say. He did suggest that during the forty-five year period preceding the Last Judgment "the Ministers as Angels, letting in the elect by conversion through the gates of particular Churches, into the community of the whole Church of New Jerusalem: shall hereby be instruments of bringing them into the heavenly perfection, and shall therein be glorified with their converts."[57]

Somewhere in between Davenport and Parker stood Thomas Shepard, the minister at Cambridge. Shepard, who was quite strict in the admission of church members, was much less certain in his views on apocalyptic matters than either Davenport or Parker. At one point, after speculating about whether one of Brightman's interpretations could be applied to the conversion of the Indians, he wrote, "but I have not skill in prophesies, nor do I beleeve every mans interpretation of such Scriptures."[58] It is not too surprising, therefore, to discover that Shepard rejected the idea of a millennial reign of

---

[56]Ibid., 124-25.

[57]Ibid., 148-49.

[58]Thomas Shepard, The Clear Sun-shine of the Gospel Breaking forth upon the Indians in New-England (London, 1648), 30.

the saints on earth, although he was still prepared to relate the New England Way to the coming of Christ. This comes out most clearly in his treatment of the parable of the ten virgins in a series of sermons preached between 1636 and 1640. A preacher who was known for his "melting" sermons on both sides of the Atlantic, Shepard was concerned in this series with the difference between the sincere Christian and "the most refined Hypocrite." To distinguish between saving and common grace was an endeavor particularly helpful to a people striving to build regenerate churches, and Shepard's work enjoyed a long popularity in New England. For our purposes, however, the context into which he put his elaborate distinction between true and false regenerations is more interesting than the distinctions themselves.

He made this context clear at the very beginning of his exposition. The parable, he said, dealt with the churches' preparation to meet with Christ and with the coming of the bridegroom Himself. Shepard thought there would be not one but two comings of Christ. The first, a figurative rather than literal appearance, would be "to call the <u>Jews</u>, and to gather in the fulness of the <u>Gentiles</u>, with them, which is called the <u>brightness of his coming</u>, <u>2 Thes. 2. 8.</u> When there shall be such a brightness of the Truth shining forth in the world, armed with such instruments as shall utterly destroy Antichrist, long before his second coming."[59] The second coming would be at the time of the Day of Judgment. The parable, therefore, could be taken as applying to either coming. Of the two, Shepard considered it more likely that it referred to the latter coming. But this did not mean that it contained no useful morals for New England, particularly since these were the days when Christ's first coming in "a brightness of the truth" was obviously wreaking havoc on Antichrist.

> So that although this Parable looks most directly unto those times which are yet to come, yet as all examples registered in holy Scripture for time past, are applicable and useful for use, so these that are yet to come, are alike

---

[59]Thomas Shepard, <u>The Parable of the Ten Virgins Opened and Applied</u> (London, 1695), Part I, 9.

instructive to us, especially in these times and places, wherein
the Lord (according to his manner of working great things
usually) gives among us some small, yet lively resemblance of
those dayes.[60]

The churches' preparation for Christ would be the same no matter
whether it was the first or the second time. They would become
"virgin-churches"--fit spouses for their holy Bridegroom.

> The state of the Members of some Churches about the time of
> Christ's coming, shall be this, they shall not be openly
> prophane, corrupt and scandalous, but Virgin-Professors,
> awakened (for some season) out of carnal security, stirring,
> lively Christians, not preserving their Chastity and Purity
> meerly in a way of works, but waiting for Christ in a
> Covenant of Grace, only some of these, and a good part of
> these, shall be indeed wise, stored with spiritual wisdom,
> fill'd with the power of Grace; but others of them, and a
> great part of them too, shall be found foolish at the coming
> of the Lord Jesus.[61]

Obviously the lesson for New Englanders in this parable was the
danger of considering themselves to be regenerate when in fact
they were naught but foolish hypocrites. To lessen this
possibility with a detailed description of the true "symptons"
of regeneration was the object of Shepard's sermons.

Of all the ministers who came to New England during the
first years of settlement, probably the most forthright exponent
of apocalyptical ideas was John Eliot, the famous missionary to
the Indians. Eliot was one of the first arrivals in
Massachusetts, landing in Boston in 1631. He was soon
established as the minister at Roxbury and remained there until
his death in 1690 at the age of eighty-six. Sometime during the
first years of his ministery, Eliot became determined to
evangelize the Indians. He hired an English-speaking Indian to
teach him the language, and was finally ready to begin his
missionary work in 1646. Eliot labored diligently for the rest

---

[60]Ibid., 9-10.

[61]Ibid., 3.

of his life among the Indians, often under very discouraging conditions. His perseverance in such a difficult work is all the more impressive since he made no concessions to Indian barbarityin the matter of church polity. The requirements for admission to membership in their churches, which were established only after years of preparation, were as high as those of the majority of the English churches.

For our purposes the most interesting thing about Eliot's missionary activity is its clearly apocalyptic inspiration. In the numerous letters Eliot wrote to England describing the work and asking for funds, he repeatedly connects missions to the Indians with the advent of the millennium. In one letter Eliot wrote of the missions as "a day of small things," and begged for the prayers of the saints and churches. "There is [he continued] the more eminent need of Faith and Prayer, that the Lord himself, by his speciall grace, favour, and providence, would appear in this matter: for the Lord must raigne in these latter dayes, and more eminently, & observably, overtop all Instruments and meanes."[62] Just a year later in 1650, he maintained that "all those signes preceding the glorious coming of Christ are accomplishing," and announced his determination to see that the Indians "be wholly governed by the Scriptures in all things both in Church and State," since "unto that frame the Lord will bring all the world ere he hath done, but it will be more difficult in other Nations who have been adulterate with their Antichristian or humane wisdom."[63] By 1653, Eliot was convinced that the Lord had "raised and improved" Oliver Cromwell to overthrow Antichrist and informed the Protector that the conversion of the Indians confirmed the arrival of the time for the spread of Christ's Kingdom over all the world.

---

[62]John Eliot and Thomas Mayhew, Jr., The Glorious Progress of the Gospel Amongst the Indians in New England, ed. Edward Winslow (London, 1649), 18.

[63]John Eliot and Thomas Mayhew, Jr., The Light Appearing More and More Towards the Perfect Day, ed. Henry Whitfield (London, 1651), 23.

In these times the Prophesies of <u>Antichrist</u> his downfall are
accomplishing. And do we not see that the Spirit of the
Lord, by the word of Prophesie, hath raised up men,
instruments in the Lords hand, to accomplish what is written
herein . . . In like manner the Lord having said, <u>That the
Gospel shall spread over all the Earth, even to all the ends
of the Earth: and from the riseing to the setting Sun: all
Nations shal become the Nations, and Kingdoms of the Lord
and of his Christ</u>. Such words of Prophesie hath the Spirit
used to stir up the servants of the Lord to make out after
the accomplishment thereof: and hath stirred up a mighty
Spirit of Prayer, and expectation of Faith for the
Conversion both of the <u>Jewes</u>, (yea all <u>Israel</u>) and of the
<u>Gentiles</u> also, all over the world.[64]

Eliot undertook his missionary work to the Indians in the
firm conviction that these were the "latter dayes," when the
millennial Kingdom of Christ would appear and spread to the ends
of the earth. He had very definite ideas about the nature of
the coming reign of the Lord. Sometime around 1650 he wrote a
treatise entitled <u>The Christian Commonwealth: or, the Civil
Policy of the Rising Kingdom of Jesus Christ</u> which he dedicated
to "the Chosen, and Holy, and Faithful, who manage the Wars of
the Lord, against Antichrist, in great <u>Britain</u>."[65] According
to Eliot, Christ's rule on earth would not be a personal one,
but would consist simply of the supremacy of the Bible. "The
Government of the Lord Jesus, . . . by the Word of his Mouth,
written in the holy Scriptures, shall order all affairs among
men; And great shall be his Dominion: . . . all men submitting
to be ruled by the Word, in civil, as well as
Church-affairs."[66] The work of the saints, therefore, in

---

[64]John Eliot and Thomas Mayhew, Jr., <u>Tears of Repentance</u>
(London, 1653), "To the Reader."

[65]The treatise was not published until 1659 when, on the
eve of the Restoration, it caused the government of
Massachusetts Bay Colony profund embarrassment. Eliot
eventually made a public retraction.

[66]<u>The Christian Commonwealth</u> (London, 1659), "To the
Chosen, and Holy, and Faithful, etc."

84

these tumultuous days was to act as the Lord's instrument in
bringing about Christ's rule--"whether by Councils or Wars, or
otherwise." In prosecuting "that great business of changing the
Government in England," they should not search human polities
and platforms of government, but should turn to the Scripture
for "a Divine institution of civil Government."[67] The Spirit
would bless "every institution of the Word, to make it powerful
and effectual to attain its end better, and more effectually
then any Humane Ordinance and Institution in the World can
do."[68]

The polity which Eliot thought the Word of God had
instituted for the government of the world was a very simple
one. It was based on God's commandment "that a people should
enter into Covenant with the Lord to become his people, even in
their Civil Society, as well as in their Church-Society."[69]
No law, statute or judgment should be accounted valid "farther
then it appeareth to arise and flow from the Word of God."[70]
Every covenanted nation should model its government upon the
pattern of Israel set forth in the Scriptures, organizing itself
into "myriads" or basic groups consisting of ten households
each. Such "myriads" would be governed by an elected ruler who
would join with other rulers of ten in an ascending hierarchy of
councils. Thus five rulers of ten would join in a council which
would govern under an elected ruler of fifty. Twenty rulers of
fifty would form a council under a ruler of a thousand, and so
on up to a million. The actual government would be carried on
in periodic courts in which judgment out of the Scriptures would
be passed on any matter requiring attention. Anything which
could not be satisfactorily dealt with by a ruler of ten would
be referred to the higher councils. In this manner the world
would be governed only by the Word of God and would partake of
no human laws or polities.

---

[67] Ibid.

[68] Ibid.

[69] Ibid., 1.

[70] Ibid., 3.

Unfortunately Eliot did not publish his views on the kind of
"Church-Societie" appropriate to the rising Kingdom of Christ
until 1665 when he wrote the Communion of Churches, a treatise
proposing "the Way of bringing all Christian Parishes to
beParticular Reforming Congregationall Churches." In this work
he was primarily concerned with setting forth a system of church
councils which would provide a means of uniting the
Congregationalists and the Presbyterians and which would also
serve as "an eminent Preparatory to these glorious dayes (when
Christ shall be King over all the Earth)."[71] Eliot's system
of church councils was very like the platform of civil
government he had advocated earlier, except that it was based on
the number twelve instead of ten. Apart from defining "a Church
of Believers" as " a company of visible saints combined
together, with one heart, to hold Communion in all the
instituted Gospel-worship, Ordinances and Discipline,"[72] Eliot
made no statement about the admission of church members. In
1657, however, in a letter to Richard Baxter, he did recommend
extending church privileges in England to the whole
congregation, excluding only "the ignorant and prophane and
scandalous." At the same time a smaller group of saints,
"called higher by the grace of Christ," might enjoy "a more
strickt and select communion" without disrupting the rest of the
parish.[73] It is difficult to say whether Eliot was merely
advocating this measure as a temporary expedient, appropriate to
the circumstances in which the English Puritans then found
themselves, or whether he felt this would be an integral part of
"Church-Societie" during the millennium. He himself never
instituted this practice in his own church in Roxbury or in the
Indian churches, in spite of the fact that he did set up the
civil government of the Praying Indians according to his
"myriad" system. In The Christian Commonwealth he argued that
"a willing subjection of a mans self to Christ in this [civil]
Covenant, is some hopeful sign of some degree of faith in

---

[71]Communion of Churches (Cambridge, Mass., 1665), 16.

[72]Ibid., 1.

[73]Some Unpublished Correspondence of the Reverend Richard
Baxter and the Reverend John Eliot, the Apostle of the American
Indians: 1656-1682, ed., F. J. Powicke (Manchester, 1931), 25.

Christ, and love to God; and as a good preparative fora more
neer approach to Christ in Church-fellowship, and
Covenant."[74] Obviously when he wrote this, Eliot was
envisaging a restriction of church membership, though it may not
have been as strict as that employed by Davenport.

Perhaps the man who best expressed the apocalyptic
preoccupations of the first colonists, was a layman, Edward
Johnson. Johnson, a carpenter, wrote the first history of
Massachusetts Bay Colony ever to be published. Entitled The
Wonder-Working Providence of Sion's Savior in New England,
Johnson's history indicates the degree to which the apocalyptic
conception of New England's destiny had taken hold of the
imagination of the rank and file of the colonists. As its title
suggests, the history was meant to depict the triumph of Christ
over Satan in His American colony. The settlers themselves were
represented as any army called up by their Savior "for freeing
his people from their long servitude under usurping
Prelacy."[75] The army's commission was a large one. As
described by Johnson, it included instructions on the demeanor
of church officers, the behaviour of the people in the
wilderness, the kind of civil government that was to be set up,
and finally, "How the People of Christ ought to behave
themselves in War-like Discipline."[76]

The war by means of which these soldiers of Christ in New
England were to put down prelacy was part of the great battle
with Antichrist. In a chapter entitled "Of the Time of the Fall
of Antichrist, and the Increase of the Gentile Churches, Even to
the Provoking of the Twelve Tribes to Submit to the Kingdom of
Christ," Johnson, while admitting the exact time of the fall was
obscure, nevertheless maintained that it was not far away. "But

---

[74]The Christian Commonwealth, p. 3.

[75]Edward Johnson, The Wonderworking Providence of Sion's
Saviour in New England, ed. William F. Poole (Andover, Mass.,
1867), 1.

[76]Ibid., 9.

to come to the time of Antichrists fall; and all that expect it
may depend upon the certainty of it: yea it may be boldly said
that the time is come, and all may see the dawning of the day:
you that long so much for it, come forth and fight: who can
expect a victory without a battel?"[77] For those scoffers and
doubters who would not believe that the day had really come
until they could see Christ's soldiers at the gates of Rome
itself, Johnson had an easy answer. Had not the Lord said,
"Come out of her my people"? To the New England historian, this
obviously meant that Christ would come when His saints had been
assembled in good order outside the church of Antichrist.

> As it was necessary that there should be a Moses and Aaron,
> before the Lord would deliver his people and destroy Pharaoh
> lest they should be wildred indeed in the Wilderness; so now
> it was needfull, that the Churches of Christ should first
> obtain their purity, and the civill government its power to
> defend them, before Antichrist come to his finall ruine: and
> because you shall be sure the day is come indeed, behold the
> Lord Christ marshalling of his invincible Army to the
> battell: some suppose this onely to be mysticall, and not
> literall at all: assuredly the spirituall fight is chiefly
> to be attended, and the other not neglected, having a neer
> dependancy one upon the other, especially at this time.[78]

Johnson's insistence that the raison d'etre of New England was a
special part in God's plan for bringing down Antichrist suggests
that, within two decades of its founding, apocalyptic thinking
had become for a great many of the colonists an essential part
of the rationale for their new departure in Puritanism. As we
have seen, the departure which made New Englanders " sui generis
even among Puritans"[79] was their conception of the
congregational church--a church whose membership was limited to
the conspicuously regenerate and yet which functioned as the
state church for an entire political body. In the New England
mind the establishment of this particular kind of holy
commonwealth had somehow become indissolubly associated with the

---

[77]Ibid., 231.

[78]Ibid., 232.

[79]Perry Miller, The New England Mind: The Seventeenth
Century (Cambridge, Mass., 1954), 434.

realization of Christ's Kingdom in history. The very creation
of a New England Way was grounded on the assumption that not
only was the Kingdom capable of being realized within history,
but that it was the inescapable obligation of the saints as
God's instruments to work actively towards its establishment.
Even though New England's ministers did not always agree on the
best way to proceed toward this goal, they did agree that the
extraordinary times in which they lived formed the prelude to a
new age. As Richard Mather put it:

> The Amplitude, and large extent of the Kingdom of Jesus
> Christ upon Earth, when the Heathen shall be his
> Inheritance, and the uttermost parts of the Earth his
> possession: and when all Kings shall fall down unto him, and
> all Nations do him service, . . . is a thing plainly and
> plentifully foretold and promised in the Holy Scriptures; .
> . . And although as yet our Eyes have never see it so, nor
> our Fathers afore us, . . . yet the time is coming, when
> things shall not thus continue but be greatly changed and
> altered, because the Lord hath spoken this Word, and it
> cannot be that his Word should not take effect."[80]

From the very beginning, the bent of the colonists in
Massachusetts Bay--unlike their brethren at Plymouth--was not to
withdraw from the world but to reform it, to work within the
institutional continuities of history rather than to deny them.
The tremendous impulse toward purity that gave birth to New
England was gratified only on the condition that the saints
would not thereby cut themselves off from the historical
church--manifested for them in the Church of England--or from
the political power of the state. Yet the Kingdom which they as
God's instruments were pledged to further was not temporal but
spiritual. Somehow this world's institutions had to be
refashioned to conform to Christ's Spiritual Kingdom. "The
latter Erecting of Christ's Kingdom in whole Societies, . . .
was our Design, and our Interest in this Country: tho' with
Respect to the Inward and Invisible Kingdom, as the Scope
thereof."[81]

---

[80]"To the Christian Reader," in Eliot and Mayhew, Tears of
Repentance.

[81]Jonathan Mitchell, quoted in Miller, 433.

It is no wonder that most of their English contemporaries reacted to this intention with incredulity and charges of fanaticism, for the New England design was precisely to make visible that which they admitted was invisible. They set out to do nothing less than reveal the boundaries of grace by making the church conform to the inward rule of Christ in the hearts of the elect. This ambition to erect Christ's Kingdom by making it synonomous with the visible church and the definitive element of a secular community was much closer to radical millennialism than most Puritans came in the seventeenth century and ran counter to the Calvinist conception of the church and its role in the world. For Calvin although the church stood in a peculiar relationship to the Kingdom, it was identified with the Kingdom only in the sense that it served as the matrix for the embyronic, spiritual Kingdom of Christ. Only when this foetal Kingdom had been delivered from time's womb on the Last Day would its outlines be visible to the world. Then in the separation of the saved and the damned men would indeed perceive the predestined limits of grace. Until that time it was the implicit rather than the explicit growth of Christ's Kingdom which both impelled and shaped the flux of history.

In opposition to this conception of the Kingdom, the New England Puritans contended "that the visible Church of God on earth, especially in the times of the Gospel, is the Kingdom of Heaven upon earth."[82] The touchstone to the New England conception of the church lies in the qualifying phrase, "especially in the times of the Gospel." Having agreed with Calvin and their English brethren that the Kingdom grew in history toward its eventual climactic triumph, the New England Puritans went on to maintain that by means of a last preaching of grace--the Reformation--the church would become more and more clearly identified with the Kingdom as the hour of the latter's consummation approached. If the Reformation did mark God's last

---

[82]Shepard, Parable of the Ten Virgins, Part I, 4.

offer of salvation to a sinful world, it seemed logical to the
New England clergy that this offer would be an example of purity
as close to perfection as possible this side of heaven. What
the New Englanders were saying, in other words, was that a
particular church, covenanted together in "primitive" purity,
was the closest possible historical approximation of an absolute
eschatological reality. As they themselves put it:

> We still beleeve though personall Christians may be eminent
> in their growth of Christianitie: yet Churches had still
> need to grow from apparent defects to purities; aud [sic]
> from Reformation to Reformation, age after age, till the
> Lord have utterly abolished Antichrist with the breath of
> his mouth, and the brightnesse of his coming, to the full
> and cleare revelation of all his holy Truth; especially
> touching the ordering of his house and publick worship.[83]

Thus the congretational churches of New England must be
interpreted as looking forward to Judgement Day as well as
backward to the Apostolic churches and beyond them to God's
covenant with the Israelites. The churches of New England were
not merely an extension of God's transaction with Abraham, but a
representation of things to come. To conceive of the visible
church as the Kingdom of Heaven meant that each individual
church covenant was an anticipation of Judgment Day--a
miniature, albeit incomplete, sorting out of the saved and the
damned. Its plausibility ultimately depended upon the
assumption that in His last offer of grace, the Lord would so
pour out His Spirit upon the land that regenerate men would be
able to discern the workings of divine grace in the hearts of
their friends and neighbors. That regenerate men could be
fallible, New Englanders would have been the first to admit.
There would be no time before the end when the church upon earth
would be so pure, that not a hypocrite would be in it.

---

[83]John Davenport, An Answer of the Elders of the Several
Churches in New-England unto Nine Positions Sent over to Them
(London, 1643), "An Epistle Written by the Elders of the
Churches in New-England."

Yet this inability to attain perfection was no warrant for including within the Kingdom men patently unregenerate. As John Cotton put it, arguing against the contention that it was unreasonable to expect a visible church to remain undefiled, "It is not every sinne, that defileth a Church, but sin openly knowne, and allowed, at least tollerated and not proceeded against by due admonition, and censure according to the rule of the Gospell. . . . Let no man decline the evidence of this truth, by the wonted evasion of the invisible Church."[84] The covenanted saints--those who could manifest their faith in the outcome of history by binding themselves to the fulfillment of divine purpose--could exclude large numbers of their compatriots from church membership in the certainty that the Spirit of the Lord would guarantee a working percentage of truly regenerate members because these were the "daies of the coming of the Son of man, wherein the Churches (especially in these placed) grow to be Virgin-Professors."[85]

The New England Puritans--with the possible exception of John Eliot--were by no means desirous of radically reconstructing the society which had produced them; but in terms of their eschatological conception of church history, they were outright revolutionaries insofar as they thought of themselves as the instruments providence had chosen to "advance" history by making a decisive and irrevocable break with Antichristian corruptions. To say exactly when the majority of the New England Puritans arrived at this conclusion would be difficult. But as we shall see, in the second generation's nostalgia for the heroic purity of their fathers, the connection between a congregational church and the imminent coming of Christ became an inextricable part of the fabled errand into the wilderness. The validity of the vision of New England as a new chosen nation in their minds came to depend upon its position as the penultimate development in the story of man's salvation from Adam's fall to the Day of Judgment.

---

[84]John Cotton, Of the Holinesse of Church-Members (London, 1650), 95.

[85]Shepard, Parable of the Ten Virgins, Part I, 10.

Chapter IV.

THE NEW-ENGLISH ISRAEL

One of the most intriguing aspects of the Puritans in America, both for their contemporary critics and modern historians, was their compulsion to fuse the regenerate and the unregenerate into a single dedicated community while at the same time insisting upon an uncompromising separation of the saved and the damned. The reasoning that allowed them to maintain that the errand into the wilderness was a communal enterprise and yet exclude many of the people from political or ecclesiastical influence has been a puzzle now for several centuries. Critics and admirers both have been fascinated by the relative success (at least at first) which the colony's leaders enjoyed in convincing a majority of sinners that they should cheerfully submit to the political and spiritual rule of a minority of saints. One reason was undoubtedly their skill in arguing that godly magistrates in a godly commonwealth, limited "both by their church covenant and by their oath, and by the dutye of their places, to square all their proceedings by the rule of Gods word, for the advancement of the gospell and the weale publick," might rationally be presumed to be giving voice to the judgments of the Lord.[1] By identifying the same common political good with the glory of God, it could be consistently maintained that "the common welfare of all, as well in the Church as without; . . . will then most certainly be effected, when the publick Trust and Power of these matters is committed to such men as are most approved according to God; and these are Church-members."[2] Liberty for the Christian lay not in doing as he pleased but in doing his duty. A state which provided its citizens with the opportunity "to serue the Lord and worke out our Salvacion vnder the power and purity of his holy Ordinances," was adequately guaranteeing their essential

---

[1] Quoted in Miller, 424.

[2] John Davenport, _A Discourse about Civil Government in a New Plantation Whose Design is Religion_ (Cambridge, Mass.. 1663). 10.

rights.[3] The righteous state could justly claim jurisdiction over the bodies and souls of its inhabitants insofar as these were capable of external regulation.

But this brings us to an even more perplexing problem. When did a state become godly, or, to put it the other way around, by what warrant could the godly constitute themselves into a state--particularly when the largest part of the community would consist of unregenerate persons? According to their critics, the New Englanders had succeeded in creating neither a holy commonwealth nor a just state. Roger Williams attacked them for debasing religion by mixing it with civil government; while at the same time the Presbyterians were accusing the colonists of being over scrupulous by requiring freemen to be church members. It was, they said, unnecessary and unfair for New England men to exclude "free burgesses" from participation in government merely because they were not visibly regenerate.

In all justice to the founders of Massachusetts Bay Colony, however, it should be pointed out that at first they had probably not intended to exclude a substantial number of persons from civil affairs. If the practice of requiring evidence of regeneration for church membership began after 1633, then when freemanship was opened to all church members in 1631, it was most likely done on the assumption that virtually all of the colony's adult males, with the exception of servants, would be so qualified. Before sailing to the New World, Winthrop and his associates had already done everything they could to insure that those emigrating to New England would be godly Puritans. As John Davenport put it, New England had been a place "where all, or the most considerable part of first and free Planters, profess[ed] their desire and purpose of entering into Church-fellowship according to Christ, and of enjoying in that State all the Ordinances in purity and peace, and of securing the same unto their posterity, so farre as men are able."[4]

---

[3]John Winthrop, "A Modell of Christian Charity," Winthrop Papers, ed. Steward Mitchell (1931), II, 293.

[4]Davenport, A Discourse about Civil Government, 12.

Still, the "first and free Planters" in Massachusetts had chosen
to limit the franchise to church members and whether or not they
had contemplated the possibility of regenerate members, they
certainly had in mind a more godly church membership than the
one they had left behind in England. This leaves us with our
original question--why did the Puritans emigrating in 1630
consider it so important to cast their enterprise into a form
that was neither fish nor fowl, neither a completely religious
community nor a completely secular state, but something a later
generation aptly called "Christian Tribes"?

John Winthrop's famous sermon, A Modell of Christian
Charity, preached en route to the New World, is one of the best
statements of exactly what the Puritans had in mind when they
first set out to build their controversial commonwealth. To
begin with, it shows just how essential it was for them that the
great migration be that of a community and not merely the
transplantation of disparate individuals. Before they had yet
set foot in New England, Winthrop was concerned to impress upon
his fellow colonists the necessity of community. He began by
pointing out the broadest possible basis for communion among
men--"the Condicion of mankinde." God had decreed differences
among men "that every man might haue need of other, and from
hence they might be all knitt more nearly together in the Bond
of brotherly affection."[5] The necessity of exercising justice
and mercy in the communities growing out of this elemental
dependency was evident to all men by the light of nature.
Christians living under the law of the Gospel had even greater
incentives to live in communal love, for while the light of
nature "propounds one man to another, as the same fleshe and
Image of god [sic], this, [the law of the Gospel] as a brother
in Christ allsoe, and in the Communion of the same spirit and
soe teacheth vs to put a difference between Christians and
others. Doe good to all especially to the household of
faith."[6] In the same manner the law of the Gospel set forth a

---

[5]Winthrop, 283.

[6]Ibid., 284.

difference of seasons and occasions so that "community of perills calls for extraordinary liberallity and soe doth Community in some speciall seruice for the Churche."[7]

Having established both the natural and Christian foundations of community, Winthrop went on to apply these imperatives for cohesion to the situation of the emigrants. They were a people who professed themselves fellow members of Christ, and this alone was enough to bind them in bonds of brotherly love. The work which they had in hand was "by a mutuall consent through a speciall overruleing providence, and a more then an ordinary approbation of the Churches of Christ to seeke out a place of Cohabitation and Consorteshipp vnder a due forme of Government both ciuill and ecclesiasticall."[8] The aim of the work was to serve the Lord, to procure the comfort and increase of the church, and to work out salvation under God's pure ordinances. Finally, the means whereby the work was to be accomplished would have to be commensurate with its goals.

The colonists were a chosen people, marked out by divine providence for a special role, and hence not at liberty to follow ordinary means or to pursue ordinary, earthly ends in the great task ahead of them. Rather they must be "knitt together in this worke as one man, . . . allwayes haueing before our eyes our Commission and Community in the worke, our Community as members of the same body."[9] Winthrop could therefore exhort his companions to the practice of communal love and mutual forbearance on the multiple grounds of their status as men, as Christians, and, most important, as Christians engaged in a special service for the church. By undertaking this special service, the colonists had voluntarily entered into a covenant with God. Winthrop reminded them that the Lord would hold them strictly to account. If they failed in creating a model of

---

[7] Ibid.

[8] Ibid., 293.

[9] Ibid., 294.

Christian charity in the New World, they would surely perish out
of their promised land; but, on the other hand, if they
succeeded, God would "delight to dwell among vs, as his owne
people and will commaund a blessing vpon vs in all our
wayes."[10]

It is apparent from Winthrop's sermons that the commission
the Puritans had been given was inconceivable to them apart from
a special kind of community. A "due forme of Government" in
civil as well as ecclesiastical matters was patently necessary
for its successful prosecution. But if the purity of the Lord's
ordinances could not be attained outside the context of a
covenanted community, bound by specific profession to serve the
Lord, it was precisely this special service for the church which
in turn gave the community its principles of cohesion. Although
any nation which professed God's ordinances was to some degree
in covenant with the Lord, not every nation could enjoy a
special covenantal relationship. Special covenants were limited
to those people whom God had chosen to exemplify His truth at
crucial points in history. Such elect nations were
distinguished by the surpassing and universal significance of
the role they played in the story of redemption. Israel, of
course, was the most obvious example of a chosen nation. For
the Puritans others would have been the Waldensians and the

---

[10]Ibid. Perhaps the closest equivalent to Winthrop's
sermon in the Plymouth colony is Robert Cushman, A Sermon
Preached at Plimmoth in New-England (London, 1622). Cushman's
sermon, which was preached in December, 1621, also stressed the
need for brotherly love and mutual help in the new colony. Yet
though Cushman told the colonists they had "couenanted here to
cleaue together in the seruice of God, and the King," he set
forth no large, overriding commission as did Winthrop.

Albigensians,[11] Germany in Luther's time, Calvin's Geneva, and Elizabethan England. Each had taken its turn at exemplifying some portion of God's truth in its progressive recovery from antichristian corruption. But now that truth, the daughter of time, looked to be driven out of Europe altogether, it seemed clear that God had chosen New England as her residence--possibly until the end of time.[12]

In order, therefore, that history might progress to its predestined consummation, God had sifted a nation for professing, though not necessarily regenerate persons. These people He had bound to Himself, to each other, and to the pursuit of a special destiny by means of a communal covenant. He had dispatched them across a "vast ocean" to settle in a new promised land. The initial and continuing success of the colony was His seal upon the national covenant. To later generations it seemed that this "ratification" had by implication guaranteed the cosmic significance of New England's historic role. If successful, the New-English Israel, just as much as its ancient

---

[11]The Puritan conception of the Waldensians and Albigensians was largely based on Jean Perrin, Histoire des Vaudois (Geneva, 1619), translated into English by Samson Lennard as Luthers Forerunners: or, A Cloud of Witnesses Deposing for the Protestant Faith (London, 1624). This work depicts the Waldensians and Albigensians as prototype Protestants, valiantly battling antichristian corruption. Winthrop referred to them in passing as examples of brotherly love in A Modell of Christian Charity. A good discussion of the New England Puritan image of the Waldensians is found in Giorgio Spini, "Riforma Italiana e Mediazioni Ginevrine nella Nuova Inghilterra Puritana," Ginevra e l'Italia (Florence, 1959).

[12]See Thomas Hooker, The Danger of Desertion (London, 1641). Hooker preached this sermon immediately before leaving for New England in 1633.

prototype, would be the guardian, preserver, and exemplar of
God's truth in a corrupt world. As such it would be related
directly to the Lord as the Lord of history in a manner which no
profane nation could ever hope to emulate. As Winthrop put it,
"wee shall finde that the God of Israell is among vs, when tenn
of vs shall be able to resiste a thousand of our enemies, when
hee shall make vs a prayse and glory, that men shall say of
succeeding plantacions: the lord [sic] make it like that of New
England: for wee must Consider that wee shall be as a Citty vpon
a Hill, the eies of all people are vppon vs."[13]

The particular truth to which New England had been called
upon to bear witness concerned "the Kingdom and Government of
Christ in his Churches; which is the great work of this age, and
of this nick of time."[14] When Winthrop set forth his model of
Christian charity, he probably did not believe that Christ's
government in His churches entailed the restriction of
membership to the visibly regenerate. In 1630 the colonists
could have fulfilled their covenant with the Lord by gathering
congregational churches out of well-behaved people who professed
a "historical" faith, by seeing that these churches exercised
discipline in accordance with the Bible, and by electing
magistrates who would support the churches and do their best to
repress known sin. All of these things were quite clearly
within the power of any well-intentioned people who had been
blest with the opportunity to build a Christian commonwealth
from scratch--especially if they enjoyed God's special favor.
Winthrop had already explained this point in answer to
objections that if New England were to succeed at all, it would
only be by miraculous means: "Though miracles be now ceased yet
men may expecte a more then ordinarie blessing from God vpon all

---

[13]Winthrop, 294-95.

[14]John Allin and Thomas Shepard, "The Preface . . . before
Their Defence of the Answer Made unto the Nine Questions,"
Massachusetts, or the First Planters of New-England, the End and
Manner of Their Coming Thither, and Abode There (Boston, 1696),
29.

lawfull meanes where the worke is the Lords and he is sought in it according to his will, for it is vsuall with him to encrease or weaken the strenth [sic] of the meanes as he is pleased or displeased with the Instruments and the action."[15] Although it would not be easy for the colonists to live up to that fundamental requirement of all Christian communities--brotherly love--none of the articles in the Lord's commission as Winthrop had described it would be impossible to fulfill.

It was, therefore, quite logical for the people of New England to look for a providential strengthening or weakening of their means as they succeeded or failed in performing the requirements of the national covenant. God's demands clearly lay within the limits of their natural abilities; hence the responsibility for the fate of the "Citty vppon a Hill" was solely their own. Under these circumstances, the actual dispensations of providence became a matter of supreme importance for the colony. Soon after their arrival in the New World, the settlers instituted a system of fast and thanksgiving days designed to make public acknowledgment of the bearing of God's Spirit toward His people. When the General Court, taking stock of the favorable or unfavorable judgments which had recently been visited upon the land, deemed it necessary to make an official recognition of them, it issued a call for a day of thanksgiving--or more often a day of fasting. The colony's churches, at their discretion, then responded with an appropriate service. In the sermons which they preached upon these occasions, the ministers were careful to exhort the people to reform, either as a preventive against complacency or as a remedy for their provoking sins. Otherwise, they warned, New England might expect even greater judgments. As a later generation put it, "so long as there is not repentance and reformation in a people there is not likelihood that Gods wrath

---

[15]"Reasons to Be Considered, and Objections with Answers," Winthrop Papers, II, 144.

should be pacified by Judgments formerly inflicted: but rather that there will be a procedure to further, greater and sorer Judgements."[16]

In the early years of the colony, providential judgments descended predictably. The people frequented taverns, neglected the Sabbath, or concerned themselves overmuch with things of this world. Providence responded with hail, drought, Indians, or the plague. But at the same time New England was sustained through all the crises, physical and spiritual, which threatened its existence. Both the colonists and their churches prospered from the influx of immigrants fleeing Laudian persecution in ever increasing numbers. The national covenant was working precisely as Winthrop had said it would. The rule of righteous men in the interest of Christ's Kingdom did indeed insure the favor or God. By organizing their society on the premise that Christ governed the world "for his Churches sake; when that is once compleat, the world shall soon be at an end,"[17] the Puritans had come a long way toward the realization of a model of Christian charity. Nevertheless, this blessed state of affairs was doomed virtually from its inception. For when John Cotton and his fellow ministers had decided that New England churches should be the first instance of the regenerate churches prophesied by the Apocalypse, they introduced endless complications into Winthrop's straight-forward model. Men by themselves could not achieve grace, nor could God be bound by a national covenant to save the damned merely because a people professed the purity of His ordinances. If pure ordinances meant that churches should consist only of regenerate members, the power to fulfill the requirements of the national covenant had been taken from the colonists. According to the new definition of purity, they could only hope that the population of New England contained within it a sufficient number of the elect to justify the existence of a New-English Israel.

---

[16]William Adams, The Necessity of the Pouring Out of the Spirit (Boston, 1679), 11.

[17]Davenport, Discourse on Civil Government, 15.

Although they could continue to maintain a purity of outward forms, henceforward, a purity of spirit would be required of them too. For New England it was no longer true that "If . . . a people doe outwardly worship God, and sincerely mend things that be amisse, they may continue [in His presence.]"[18]

The horns of this particular dilemma were not immediately evident. If New England's apocalyptic destiny now seemed to demand a correlation between the covenant of grace and the covenant of the nation, there was every reason to suppose that such a correlation would exist. In the Apocalypse the promise of greater purity in the church was accompanied by the assurance that in the last days God would pour out His Spirit upon the world as never before so that the quota of the elect might be filled.[19] If the inevitable concomitant of Antichrist's fall were a last great preaching of grace, then New England might rightly be expected to partake of its fruits. The people to whom so many truths about the Kingdom of Christ had been imparted could properly look to the Lord to strengthen them

---

[18]Hooker, 9.

[19]G. F. Nuttall in his book The Holy Spirit in Puritan Faith and Experience (Oxford, 1946) has shown how an emphasis on the centrality of the doctrine of the Holy Spirit went hand in hand with a powerful eschatological consciousness in England between 1640 and 1660, and how the conviction that the use of ordinances would soon be superceded by Christ's appearance contributed greatly to a tolerant attitude. He attributes the popularization of this conjunction of ideas to works by Henry Archer and Robert Maton first published in 1642. However, one has only to read Nuttall's book along with William Haller's The Elect Nation to realize that an emphasis upon the Spirit and an eschatological consciousness were both present in England long before 1642. In New England, eschatological beliefs of the Puritans early became identified with the rather rigid conception of a regenerate church. This plus the early defeat of Antinomian tendencies in the Hutchinson affair and the comparative isolation of New England probably thwarted any development of the idea of toleration such as occurred in England.

"unto stedfast perseverance, in the faith, obedience, and order
of the Gospel, unto the end."[20] In this context, then, New
England's covenant with the Lord became nothing more nor less
than a prediction that in the last days of the world, God's
Spirit would be with a righteous people in unprecedented
measure--so much so that they could safely profess a purity "not
above what was before required, but above what was ordinarily
before either attained, or attended."[21] The requirement of
visible regeneracy could safely be introduced into a
commonwealth ruled by church members if one assumed that the
number of the elect was about to increase sharply. Under these
circumstances such a requirement would not be tyrannical.
Visible saints might rule the community in order that "pure
Ordinances, pure People, pure Churches," could be achieved, but
they would do so on the assumption that their ranks would grow
rapidly through the increment of newly converted elect.

Even apart from the anticipated expansion of the covenant of
grace, the colonists had reason to believe that New England
would be full of visible saints. By any interpretation of the
national covenant, they were bound to provide in full measure
the means by which men were converted. In the experience of the
Puritans, the cultivation of the forms of righteousness was
frequently followed by the realization of its substance. The
more sermons to which a man listened, the more he read and
pondered the Bible, the more he restrained himself from sinning,
the more likely he was to be converted. Working on the
principle that "the more wee indevour, the more assistance the
help wee find from [God],"[22] the Puritans could "prepare"
themselves for grace and thus hope to facilitate the operation
of the Spirit. From this point of view the national covenant
was a pledge that the unregenerate would do all within the
limits of their natural abilities to prepare for salvation.

---

[20]Samuel Torrey and Josiah Flint, "Preface" in Adams.

[21]Cotton, Of the Holiness of Church-Members, 95.

[22]Quoted in Perry Miller, The New England Mind: From
Colony to Province (Cambridge, Mass., 1953), 56.

It was a pledge made in the firm expectation that God would complete national preparation with an unprecedented work of grace.[23]

In this manner the ministers of New England redrafted the divine commission Winthrop had first elaborated in his Model of Christian Charity. They did it because of their conviction that what had hitherto been limited to individuals scattered through society would now begin to occur on such a grand scale that it would become a social as well as an individual phenomenon. The Spirit which before had been poured out in drops and trickles was now to come full flood upon the world. Its fullness would be such that only a new society, presaging the new heaven and earth, would be an adequate expression of its bounty. The national covenant and the church covenant were both functions of the expectation that the covenant of grace must now expand to the boundaries of predestination. But whereas the covenanted church already contained the fruits of this harvest, the covenanted nation was like the ripe, unreaped field whose members stood waiting for the sickle of grace.

---

[23]On the concept of preparation see ibid., 55-67 and Norman Pettit, "The Image of the Heart in Early Puritanism: The Emergence in England and America of the Concept of Preparation for Grace" (unpublished Ph.D. dissertation, Dept. of American Studies, Yale University, September, 1962). Pettit has traced a number of different attitudes among first generation ministers on the question of preparation. These ranged from the high Calvinist view of John Cotton that man is brought to salvation only through divine constraint to Peter Bulkeley's belief that the baptized may achieve salvation through preparatory acknowledgement of God's promises to the "covenant seed." Either conception was compatible with New England's obligation to correlate the covenant of grace with the covenant of the nation, although Cotton's view would obviously emphasize divine initiative in an outpouring of grace, while Bulkeley's would give a larger role to the efforts of the people themselves.

104

Ultimately the basis for the New Englanders' unholy (as
their critics saw it) ambition for righteousness was a belief in
God's will to end the reign of Antichrist rather than confidence
in their own capabilities. Once situated in the New World, they
had only to maintain themselves at the point at which they had
begun in order to satisfy the requirements of their special
commission. This, however, was easier said than done. A people
who professed purity remained subject to sins which had appeared
less serious in more profane nations. Foremost among these sins
was carnal security. Thomas Shepard categorically warned his
congregation that "in the last days Carnal Security either is or
will be the universal sin of Virgin Churches."[24] Free from
inward pain, blessed with a great plentitude of spiritual means,
and weary with long striving after Christ, such churches had the
strongest provocations to security. New England, he said,
should take heed of its peril in this direction.

> Let us therefore now examine whether this sin be not our sin
> in this Country, if it be not begun among us; . . . if we be
> Virgin-Churches, then make search if this be not our sin; we
> have all our beds and lodgings provided, the Lord hath made
> them easie to us; We never looked for such days in
> New-England, the Lord hath freed us from the pain and
> anguish of our Consciences; we have Ordinances to the full,
> Sermons too long, and Lectures too many, and private
> meetings too frequent, a large profession many have made,
> but are you not yet weary? if weary, not sleepy, not
> slumbering? it may be on you before you are aware, and you
> not know it; and when so it is, it may be so sweet that you
> may be loth to see it, that so you may forsake it.[25]

The first generation had no difficulty in interpreting the
undeniable tendency of New Englanders to fall into a state of
spiritual deadness as an added indication of the lateness of the
age. Their greatest fear was that they would be unable to
sustain the purity of their reformation until history was ripe

---

[24]Parable of the Ten Virgins, Part II, 2.

[25]Ibid., 5.

for its appointed consummation. If New England were not aroused from its carnal sleep before the end, there would be not room for its virgin churches in the heavenly bridal chamber. Then too, there was always the possibility that the end was further off than the first divines had anticipated. Acknowledging that "it may be the last and great coming of the Lord is not very nigh (although we are doubtless in the last times,)"[26] Shepard warned his contemporaries against "letting a new Generation of Harlots into Christs bosom, I mean, not greatly caring for Posterity, that they may know and serve this God, for after this Generation is past, our children are to follow, and 'tis very rare that they prove right, yet it may be so."[27] If the fervor of the early years had to be stretched beyond the span of a generation, it was not only possible but perhaps even probable that the regenerate church order would collapse under the weight of its own purity.

The men who first formulated the New England Way were perfectly well aware that it would function satisfactorily only in a society in which the "total quantity" of godliness was constantly increasing. On the assumption that this would be the case not only in New England but throughout the world from their time forward, they had initiated the practise of requiring evidence of regeneration for church membership. At the same time, however, they had continued to baptize the infant children of church members, thus bringing them within the membership of the church. Since these children--however godly their parents--were clearly not yet regenerate, they were not admitted to the Lord's Supper until they had actually experienced an "effectual calling." Full membership was delayed in the expectation that the children of saints would one day partake of the Lord's grace in their own right. "These church-members that were so born, . . . have many privileges which others (not church-members) have not: they are in covenant with God; have

---

[26]*Ibid.*, Part I, 29.

[27]*Ibid.*, 38.

the seale thereof upon them, viz. Baptisme; & so if not
regenerated, yet are in a more hopefull way of attayning
regenerating grace, & all the spiritual blessings both of the
covenant & seal."[28]

This infant baptism represented a fundamental inconsistency
in the New England Way. To admit members into regenerate
churches by birth alone implied either that such children were
destined to be saved by virtue of their parentage alone, or that
children who failed to become regenerate upon reaching maturity
would be expelled in order to maintain the purity of the
church.[29] If, as actually happened, the second generation
were neither converted nor expelled, then the question of the
status of _their_ children was bound to come up.[30] The fact
that the founders neglected to face up to the inconsistencies
implicit in requiring both a regenerate membership and infant
baptism--in spite of their oft repeated doubts about the piety
of the next generation--suggests that they expected the

---

[28]The Cambridge Platform, 1648 in Williston Walker, _The
Creeds and Platforms of Congregationalism_ (New York, 1893), 224.

[29]It is noteworthy that the first alternative is not
incompatible with Peter Bulkeley's emphasis upon the role of
acknowledgment of the covenant in achieving salvation and his
conception of the efficacy of baptism. Bulkeley also held very
liberal views on the admission of church members.

[30]On the problem of baptism see Morgan, 113-138.

millennium to begin before a third generation of New Englanders appeared to pose the problem.[31] Most of them did believe that some sort of eschatological crisis would be reached around 1650, and the course of English history in the 1640's could hardly have undermined their apocalyptic expectations. It is, therefore, significant that the men who drafted the Cambridge Platform between 1646 and 1648 equivocated on the question of baptism. If 1650 were to initiate a new age in heaven and on earth, then there was obviously no need to decide the worrisome question of whether or not the children of baptized but as-yet-unregenerate church members should themselves be baptised. By 1662, the problem could no longer be avoided. Whether or not history was about to end, a third generation had already arrived. Some decision had to be reached about their relationship to the church. In that year the ministers once again met in a synod and this time produced the Halfway Covenant, which permitted the as-yet-unregenerate members to transmit church membership and baptism to the children, provided they reaffirmed their historical faith and promised to submit to the discipline of the church.

---

[31]It is possible that John Cotton expected the children of visible saints to be converted "automatically" upon reaching maturity during the millennium. As we have seen, Cotton thought all of those who were not within regenerate churches at the beginning of the thousand years would be unable to enter them for the duration. Since he did not believe that the saints would be immortal during this period, the only possible means of continuing the church's existence on earth would be through the regular "automatic" conversion of the "seed of the covenant." In 1641 a sermon preached by Cotton was noted by John Winthrop in his journal in the following entry: "Mr. Cotton out of that in Revelation 15. none could enter into the temple until, &c. delivered, that neither Jews nor any more of the Gentiles should be called until Antichrist were destroyed, viz. to a church estate, though here and there a proselyte." The History of New England, ed. James Savage (Boston, 1825), II, 30. If Cotton could postulate such a state of affairs in the relatively short period before Antichrist's fall, it is more than likely that he visualized a virtually "tribal" church during the millennium. As early as 1634, he approved the baptism of a child of unconverted parents whose grandfather was a church member. See Walker, 251.

The Halfway Covenant settled the question of the formal
relationship of the founders' grandchildren to the church, but
as everyone knew, it had not touched the heart of what had
become New England's greatest problem, declension. It was
obvious that if the second generation had experienced the saving
faith of their fathers, the baptism of the third generation
would have presented no difficulty. It is true that unless <u>all</u>
of the children of the first church members had been converted,
the question of baptism would still have risen at some point to
plague New England. But it is also true that if the problem had
arisen in connection with only a few cases, it would hardly have
aroused the passions it did. By the 1660's the population of
New England contained distressingly few visible saints for a
holy nation. This paucity was apparent among the descendants of
the original church members as well as among the people at
large.

The real question was why regeneration had not been keeping
pace with the expanding population. Since only divine grace
could regenerate men, the lack of visible saints had to be
attributed first of all to a withdrawal of God's Spirit from the
land. But if God were no longer pouring out His Spirit upon His
chosen people, what would happen to their special work for the
church? How would they be able to maintain God's ordinances if
He did not provide them with saints to fill their pure
churches? Could it be that the architects of the New England
Way had been mistaken in their belief that these were the last
days and that the flight into the wilderness actually had no
apocalyptic significance? Understandably, the Puritans were
reluctant to answer this last question in the affirmative.
After struggling to establish and maintain a holy commonwealth
for more than three decades, they were hardly prepared to admit
that this was not what God had meant them to do in their
promised land. Nevertheless for some reason the Lord had cleary
turned His countenance away from the New-English Israel. The

colonists could only conclude they had somehow broken faith with
Him.[32]

This, at least, was the opinion of the General Court when it
first took official notice of the departure of God's Spirit. In
1652 the deputies, calling for a fast day, had included among
the more visible tokens of divine displeasure "the wordly
mindedness, oppression, & hardhartedness feared to be among
us."[33] Instead of merely sending a poor crop, tempests, or an
epidemic to indicate His wrath and the necessity of reformation,
the Lord had withdrawn His spiritual bounty from a nation sunk
deep into degeneracy. Security and folly in the daily struggle
with sin were to be expected among a people who had a surfeit of
spiritual blessings, but "worldly mindedness, oppression, &
hardhartedness" were something else again. They were the
besetting sins of a generation too preoccupied with material
gains to be wholly dedicated to heavenly salvation. The

---

[32]In "The Image of the Heart in Early Puritanism," Norman
Pettit has suggested that one of the reasons for the paucity of
church members was that an emphasis on preparatory experiences
of an extensive nature was combined with a strict admissions
policy--a combination of requirements which set an impossibly
high standard of piety. (See p. 212) While this combination
represented the views of Cotton on Church membership, it was
also a triumph for "Preparationists" such as Bulkeley since it
emphasized the role of natural abilities in the achievement of
salvation. This view obviously increased the responsibility of
New Englanders for the lack of church members, because according
to the preparationists, man could play an active part in this
regeneration. Yet, as Pettie has shown, John Norton's critical
analysis of preparation in The Orthodox Evangelist (London,
1657) undercut this view. By 1662 when the Synod adopted
Norton's ideas, the high Calvinist doctrine of divine initiative
was again prevalent. Thus the initiative in salvation was once
more taken from man and returned to God.

[33]Quoted in Miller, From Colony to Province, 28.

110

proclamation issued in 1652 was not the last one to cite
spiritual disorders as signs of God's anger. On the contrary
it was the first of many. Within the next ten years it had
become apparent that unless something were done about the
declension that was both cause and effect of the Lord's wrath,
New England that might cease to be a chosen nation. When the
second generation compared its precarious position with that of
their fathers, they could not help but be concerned. Even in
terms of Winthrop's conception of the national covenant, the
colonists had not fulfilled the obligations of a chosen people.
Before New England could expect to enjoy once more "a glorious
dispensation of the Spirit and grace of God," they had to
demonstrate they had not ceased to seek God's Kingdom. New
England's reinstatement in divine favor--the visible
manifestation of which would be an increase in the number of
regenerate church members--seemed to depend upon the people's
willingness to embark upon a more strenuous pursuit of corporate
righteousness.

In scores of jeremiads preached throughout the land, the
responsibility for the ultimate fate of the New-English Israel
was placed squarely in the hands of the people themselves. God
would dispense that bounty of the Spirit which was the sine qua
non of purity only to a nation which hungered and thirsted after
rightousness. If the colonists persisted in sinning, they were
willfully blocking the revival of the power of godliness
necessary for the resuscitation of New England's special
destiny. The remedy was simple enough: "Let every one endeavor
to get the Spirit for himself, and so there would be a general
pouring out of the spirit."[35] Moreover, the conseuqences of
failure were equally simple: "If you do not get the Spirit of
God to be in you, you will be like to be guilty of New Englands
ruine."[36] "And what a dreadful thing will it be to have the

---

[34]Samuel Torrey and Josiah Flint, "Preface" in Adams.

[35]Ibid., 36.

[36]Ibid., 40.

spoiling of such a blessed work as God hath here begun, to ly at
our door?"[37]   The imperative was clear cut; the consequences
of failure were ominous; the ultimate value of the effort was
immeasurably great.   Yet the colonists willfully pursued their
material interests with ever greater vigor and God's wrath beat
against the land in increasing waves of hard-heartedness, sin,
and carnal security.

In 1662 Michael Wigglesworth published two poems, God's
Controversy with New England and The Day of Doom.   The former
was a lamentation over New England's declension from purity, and
the latter was a description of the Great Day of Judgment in
ballad form--obviously designed for popular consumption.
Whether the author intended it or not, the juxtaposition of
these two works pointed out a possible solution to the colony's
developing spiritual dilemma.   If the explication of
providential judgments upon the whole community would not serve
to turn the populace from its pursuit of worldly advantage, then
perhaps a vivid portrayal of the eternal judgment that was in
store for each man would suffice to set individuals pondering on
the necessity of an early concern for their personal salvation.
To put it another way, self-interest has always been a more
powerful motive than patriotism, even if patriotism was invoked
in the name of a holy experiment.   From the overall point of
view the results would be the same.   Moreover, such preaching
would help reinforce New England's eschatological image of
itself.

Wigglesworth had not been the first to hit upon this idea.
In his sermons on the parable of the ten virgins (which were not
published until 1660), Thomas Shepard had observed that the
first sign of carnal security was the loss of "all fear of the
wrath to come, and the terror of God another day; . . . Many
Christians lose the sense of Gods love, yet the Lord keeps them
in the sense of his anger, and so they are awake; but when both
are gone, or this is gone, then there is and cannot but be the
first security."[38]   There was, however, "one special way to

---

[37]Ibid., 41.

[38]Parable of the Ten Virgins, Part II, 15.

prevent and remove security when it is fallen upon the hearts of
any, and that is by daily setting before you the coming of the
Lord; . . . Make the coming of the Lord real, see it real, set
it really (as it shall be) before your eyes."[39] "If God
intends mercy to you, the thoughts of these things willawaken
you, you shall see them really; if not they shall awaken you by
feeling of them."[40] Everybody in short would profit from a
due consideration of Judgment Day.

Once begun, the inclination to remind their congregations of
the joys of the blessed and the terrors of the damned at the
Last Day gradually became a habit with the ministers. In 1664
only two years after the publication of Wigglesworth's poems,
Samuel Whiting presented an extremely long compilation of sermon
notes on the Day of Judgment. Two of his colleagues, John
Wilson and Jonathan Mitchell, indicated their approval of the
subject matter in a preface that could not have spelled out more
clearly the goal at which the clergy were aiming: "And it is
observable that Divine Providence hath so disposed, that two or
three Treatises should be published among us looking this way,
as intimating that We in this wilderness where wordly cares and
pleasures are apt to overcharge us, have more then ordinary need
of that warning, to take heed of forgetting this great Day of
our Lord's second Coming, and to Watch and Pray alwayes as
preparation thereunto."[41] The rest of the second generation
was not backward in picking up the hint that their illustrious
predecessor, Mr. Shepard, had dropped. Among the most aspiring
was young Increase Mather, who, typically divining the trend of
the times, made his debut in print with The Mystery of Israel's
Salvation--a learned treatise devoted to clarifying the calling
of the Jews in "these latter ages." A few years later he did
himself one better by combining a jeremiad and a "doomsday"
sermon in The Day of Trouble is Near. After that Mather sermons
and treatises (both those of Increase and his son Cotton) on the
Day of Judgment followed one another with rapidly.

---

[39]Ibid., 28.

[40]Ibid., 29.

[41]"To the Reader" in Samuel Whiting, A Discourse of the
Last Judgment (Cambridge, 1664).

The Mathers, as might be expected of such devotees of the dreams of their forefathers, were unusual in the extent of their preoccupation with the end of time. Although other New England ministers did not go to the same extremes, the motif of the Great Judgment was increasingly worked into the fabric of their sermons. Time and again they urged their auditors to "get an interest in Christ" in preparation for the Last Day. As Samuel Whiting put it, "get a sure Portion and Interest in him; and if he that is to be your Judge, be your Saviour, this great Day, and the great transactions then, will not be dreadful to you."[42] Otherwise, if you choose to "grapple with Everlasting Burnings and will be trying Mastery with the Omnipotent One; if you provoke the Lord to anger, and think to be stronger than he, . . . and let Heaven, and all the joyes and City-priviledges of it, go for a thing of nought: Then I have no more to say but this to you. My Soul shall weep in secret places for you." These and like warnings, Whiting conjectured, "might be very advantageous to draw men seriously to Repent."[43] By 1686 Increase Mather could confirm his guess. In a preface to one of his sermons, he carefully explained that nothing had a greater tendency to waken unto repentance than serious thought of the Day of Judgment and the infinite danger in delaying conversion. Those whose ministeries had been particularly blessed by conversions, he pointed out, had had greatest success with discourse on the dangers of deferring repentance.[44]

In this manner the portrayal of the individual judgment each person would undergo at the end of time was gradually coupled with the explication of the Lord's providential judgments against the entire land. At first it was a minor theme, usually incorporated in jeremiads, but it grew in importance with every performance of that complex exercise in communal repentance--the fast day. As New England's apostasy from the purity of its founders became more and more obvious, the preoccupation with judgment--universal or parochial, individual or social--acted perhaps as a means of easing a heavy burden of guilt. Samuel Hooker must have been speaking for all those charged with New

---

[42]Ibid., "To the Christian Reader."

[43]Ibid.

[44]Increase Mather, Greatest Sinners, "Preface."

England's spiritual welfare when he voiced this slightly wistful
hope at the end of a typical jeremiad: "Truly we have had time
wherein to experience the naughtiness of our own hearts, how
bent we are to backslide and go off from God, as also our
weakness and utter insufficiency of all means in themselves
considered to keep us with God or reduce us to him when turned
away: But it may be Christ will shortly come down, and then all
will be mended. . .Let us seek him therefore till he comes, for
he loveth Righteousness, and hath not forsaken them that seek
him."[45]

Although he probably did not intend it to be such, Hooker's
statement might well be read as a confession that the errand
into the wilderness had failed. By 1677 New England had indeed
experienced the "utter insufficiency of all means in themselves
considered" to fulfill its special commission. Neither
jeremiads nor doomsday sermons nor filial piety were adequate
substitutes for the grace-full bounty of God's Spirit in a
society which aspired to "pure Ordinances, pure People, pure
Churches." From the very beginning the structure of church and
state in New England had presupposed a correlation between the
possession of godliness and the exercise of political and
religious power. Although they interpreted the requirement
differently, both Winthrop and Cotton had assumed that godly men
would control the affairs of church and state. Only on this
basis could they consider New England a chosen nation--a people
destined to foreshadow the imminent fruition of God's purpose in
history. By defining a godly man as one who had experienced
regeneration, Cotton had made the very functioning of New
England's government, both civil and ecclesiastical, dependent
upon God's intention to end history quickly. When 1650 came and
went and history had not ended, when the Halfway Covenant made
it painfully clear that second-generation New Englanders were

---

[45]Righteousness Rained from Heaven (Cambridge, Mass.,
1677), 28.

not experiencing regeneration, when, in short, the proportion of saints to the rest of the colonists became dangerously low for a holy commonwealth, New Englanders could only hope that Christ would "shortly come down" and mend all. Otherwise it was likely that their destiny in the wilderness would be merely to extend the bounds of the English realm and not to realize the Kingdom of Heaven on earth.

Chapter V.

THE WILDERNESS

In the Bible a constantly recurring motif is withdrawal into
a wilderness for the preservation of purity. The Israelites
escaped the corruption and oppressions of Egypt in the
wilderness of Sinai; in Revelation the woman flies "from the
face of the serpent" to a wilderness sanctuary; Christ Himself
withdrew into a wilderness that His purity might be tested and
thereby preserved. But, as the last example suggests, the
biblical wilderness is a place of temptations as well as a place
of refuge. "Harden not your heart, as in the provocation, and
as in the day of temptation in the wilderness."[1] Temptations,
if not overcome, can change the wilderness from a sanctuary and
a potential paradise into a barren and fearsome desert. "He
turneth rivers into a wilderness, and the watersprings into dry
ground; a fruitful land into barrenness for the wickedness of
them that dwell therein. He turneth the wilderness into a
standing water, and dry ground into watersprings. And there he
maketh the hungry to dwell, that they may prepare a city for
habitation."[2] Throughout Christian history the miraculous
metamorphosis of the wilderness into a refuge and a garden of
the Lord and the equal precariousness of the garden, which may
at any moment be reduced to a desert wilderness, have been
compelling images for God's people.[3]

For the American Puritans the ambivalent possibilities of
the wilderness for a Christian people were very real.
Confronted with the overwhelming presence of a physical
wilderness, they were deeply impressed from the beginning of

---

[1] Psalm 95:8.

[2] Psalm 107:33-36.

[3] See George H. Williams, "The Wilderness and Paradise in
the History of the Church," Church History, XXVIII (March,
1959), 3-24.

their venture with both the potential dangers and rewards of
their new home. Even before they arrived in the New World, John
Cotton instructed the colonists on the various possibilities
inherent in their position as a new chosen nation abiding in a
wilderness. In a farewell sermon preached before Winthrop's
group sailed to New England in 1630, Cotton informed his
listeners that those whom God "planted" in a new land, He would
maintain. "What hee hath planted he will maintaine, every
plantation his right hand hath not planted shalbe rooted up, but
his owne plantation shall prosper, & flourish."[4] The
colonists' condition in the wilderness would depend upon whether
or not they were a "plantation" of God. Cotton naturally was
sure that Masschusetts Bay Colony would be such a plantation.
The colonists could "plainly see a providence of God leading
from one Country to another."[5] Like the woman in Revelation
who had been given "two wings of a great eagle" to fly into the
wilderness, the settlers, "though they met with many
difficulties, yet [God] carried them high above them all, like
an eagle, flying over seas and rockes, and all hinderances."[6]
Since they were truly God's people, then, the new inhabitants of
the American wilderness would have ample reason to regard it as
a promised land.

> Others take the land by his providence, but Gods people take
> the land by promise: And therefore the land of Canaan is
> called a land of promise. Which they discerne, first, by
> discerning themselves to be in Christ, . . . Secondly, by
> finding his holy presence with them, ... And that is
> when he giveth them the liberty and purity of his
> Ordinances. It is a land of promise, where they have
> provision for soule as well as for body.[7]

---

[4]John Cotton, Gods Promise to His Plantation (London,
1630), 20.

[5]Ibid., 3.

[6]Ibid.

[7]Ibid., 6.

Cotton made clear the wilderness would function as a refuge and a potential promised land only on a provisional basis. "If you rebell against God, the same God that planted you will also roote you out againe, for all the evill which you shall doe against your selves."[8] So long as the Puritan purpose remained "the injoyment of Christ in his pure Ordinances," and only that long, could the colonists expect the barren wilderness to bloom--spiritually and materially--beneath their hands.

When the Puritans actually arrived in New England, one of the first wilderness tests they confronted was the Indian. Nothing better exemplified the ambivalent manner in which the Puritans perceived the wilderness than their reaction to its savage inhabitants. Naturally the colonists were committed to converting the Indians. This had been one of the reasons they used to procure a charter from King Charles. John Cotton had even asked, "who knoweth whether God have reared this whole Plantation for such an end."[9] Yet when the colonists actually came into contact with the Indian, they were appalled by the difficulties they would face in bringing him to a state of civilization--let alone Christianity. In the eyes of the Puritans the Indians were almost unbelievably barbarous. Though human beings, they lived in conditions little better than animals. Their food was barely palatable; their houses were huts; and their clothes were made of rude skins and furs. They slept crowded together on planks and thin mats, plagued by lice and fleas. Furthermore, they were completely unlettered in the arts and sciences. The men occupied themselves with hunting and left the women to carry on agriculture and care for all the household needs. Clearly the first settlers were "compassed about with a helplesse and idle people, the natiues of the Countrey, which cannot in any comely or comfortable manner help themselues, much lesse vs."[10] Bringing these savages to Christianity was bound to be difficult, "not only in respect of the language, but also in respect of their barbarous course of

---

[8]Ibid., 17.

[9]Ibid., 19-20.

[10]Cushman, 14.

life and poverty; there is not so much as meat, drink or lodging for them that go unto them to preach among them, but we must carry all things with us, and somewhat to give to them."[11] To these Christ would come "rich, potent, above them in learning, riches, and power; and they shall flock unto the Gospel, thereby to receive externall beneficence and advancement, as well as spirituall grace and blessings."[12]

Nevertheless, the Puritans were convinced that the Indians as human beings, however barbarous, possessed those faint glimmerings of reason known as the light of nature. "Their outsides say they are men, their actions they say [sic] are reasonable. As the thing is, so it operateth. Their correspondence of disposition with us, argueth all to be of the same constitution, and the sons of Adam, and that we had the same matter, the same mould. Only art and grace have given us that perfection which yet they want, but may perhaps be as capable thereof as we."[13] An encouragement to their conversion was "the notable reason, judgement, and capacitie that God hath given unto many of them; as also their zealous enquiring after true happinesse."[14] Theoretically the Indians were not inferior in intellectual faculties or human sensibilities to men then living in England. As descendants of Adam they possessed minds, souls, and bodies equivalent in every respect to those of Europeans. Like the wilderness in which they lived, the Indians were capable of being converted from barbarity to Christian civilization. When some of them despaired of ever becoming like the English, John Eliot told

---

[11]Eliot and Mayhew, The Glorious Progress of the Gospel, 10.

[12]Ibid.

[13]Philip Vincent, "A True Relation of the Late Battell Fought in New England between the English and the Pequet Salvages," Collections of the Massachusetts Historical Society 3rd series, V (1836), 34.

[14]Eliot and Mayhew, The Glorious Progress of the Gospel, 3.

them there were but two differences between them and the
colonists--the English prayed and served God and they worked at
planting and building, while the Indians did neither.

Until he was civilized and converted, however, the Indian
was a barbarian. So long as he remained in his unenlightened
state, he was a threat to the settlements--a visible
manifestation of the destructive potentialities of the
wilderness for an ungodly people. In some ways the combined
promise and threat of the Indian was even more disturbing for
the Puritans than the wilderness itself. For the Indian was the
human embodiment of the "wilderness-condition"--
wild, brutish, yet encompassed within God's love by virtue of
his humanity. Perhaps for the righteous men of New England an
even greater wilderness danger than that of mere physical
destruction, the possibility of degeneration, lay in the
Indian's barbarity. He was a continual reminder of what man
would be without the benefit of the Word of God.

Clearly the Indian like the physical wilderness had to be
improved and made fruitful if the Puritans were to flourish in
their sanctuary. Even apart from this consideration, the
conversion of the Indians played an important role in the
apocalyptic expectations of the first colonists. John Eliot was
not the only New Englander who linked their conversion with the
rising Kingdom of Christ. As early as 1621, the apocalyptic
significance of the Indians had been propounded by the Pilgrims,
significantly enough in conjunction with the flight of the woman
into the wilderness.

If the time be come, or shall come (as who knoweth) when
Sathan shall be let loose, to cast out his flouds against
them [God's people], here is a way opened for such as haue
wings to flie into this Wildernesse; and as by the
dispersion of the Iewish Church thorow persecution, the Lord
brought in the fulnesse of the Gentiles, so who knoweth,
wether now by tyrannie, and affliction, . . . he will not by
little and little chase them, even amongst the Heathens,
that so a light may rise vp in the darke, and the kingdome

of heauen be taken from them which now haue it, and giuen to a people that shall bring forth the fruit of it.[15]

Three years before Eliot began preaching to the Indians, Henry Dunster solicited support for missionary work (and the new college) by citing the "apprehension which many godly and wise have conceived, and that from some Scriptures compared, and from other grounds, and passages of Providence collected that (as it's very probable) God meanes to carry his Gospel westward, in these latter times of the world."[16]   By 1652 New England missions were being commended on the ground that they were fulfilling the promise that all the kingdoms of the earth should be Christ's.   "This wee hope may be but the first fruits of those great Nations unto Christ, . . . Let no man despise the day of small things, the Lord hath opened a great doore, which we hope Satan shall never be able any more to shut."[17]

The apocalyptic connotations of the Indians were reinforced for the Puritans by the speculation that their savage neighbors were descendants of the Lost Tribes of Israel--one of the many theories then current to explain the origin of the Indians.   In 1650 this theory was strengthened by the publication of Spes Israelis by Manasseh ben Israel of Amsterdam, a book which purported to give proof that the Indians were really Jews. Thomas Thorowgood followed this up two years later with his Jewes in America, which listed fifty parallels in the customs, languages, and beliefs of the two peoples.   Puritans in both Old and New England were much taken with these two books because, if the Indians were really Jews, their conversion could be related to the prophesied conversion of Israel.   In pamphlets written to

---

[15]Anon., "To His Loving Friends, the Adventurers for New-England" in Cushman. Cf. Rev. 12:14, 15. "And to the woman were given two wings of a great eagle, that she might fly into the wilderness. . . . And the serpent cast out of his mouth water as a flood after the woman.

[16]"New England's First Fruits" in Samuel E. Morison, The Founding of Harvard College (Cambridge, Mass., 1935), 430.

[17]Henry Whitfield, Strength Out of Weaknesse (Sabin Reprints; New York, 1865), "To the Reader."

promote the work of conversion, the arguments for the Jewish origins of the Indians were presented frequently. Edward Winslow, writing in 1649, was convinced that the savages were of the stock of Abraham, "especially considering the juncture oftime wherein God hath opened their hearts to entertain the Gospel, being so nigh the very years, in which many eminent and learned Divines, have from Scripture grounds, according to their apprehensions foretold the conversion of the <u>Jewes</u>."[18] Since both the conversion of the Jews and the spread of the gospel to the uttermost ends of the earth were prophesied for the beginning of the millennium, the colonists could interpret the Indian converts either as the first fruits of the accomplishment of the "fulness of the Gentiles" or as the beginning of the conversion of the Jews. Thomas Shepard was of the opinion that if Brightman's interpretation of Daniel's prophecy was true, namely, that in 1650 the eastern Jews would shake the Turk's hold from their land and regain it after a forty year struggle, "I shall hope then that these Westerne <u>Indians</u> will soon come in, and that these beginnings are but preparatives for a brighter day then we yet see among them, wherein East & West shall sing the song of the Lambe."[19] Whatever the case, he and many others were certain that "God is at work among these; and it is not usual for the Sune to set as soon as it begins to rise."[20]

Considering how momentous the consequences of Indian conversion might be for the fruition of history, the Puritans were surprisingly slow to take up missionary work. In 1630 John Cotton had enjoined the settlers to "make them [the Indians] partakers of your precious faith: as you reape their temporalls, so feede them with your spiritualls."[21] But during the next decade the pressing necessity of establishing a godly

---

[18]"To the Right the Honourable the Parliament of England," in Eliot and Mayhew, <u>The Glorious Progress of the Gospel</u>. Both the vision of the dry bones in Ezekiel 37 and the references to Israel's salvation in Romans 15 were interpreted by the Puritans as predicting the conversion of the Jews before Judgment Day.

[19]Shepard, <u>Clear Sunshine</u>, 30.

[20]<u>Ibid.</u>

[21]<u>Gods Promise to His Plantation</u>, 19.

commonwealth eclipsed any pious hopes for the conversion of the natives. Then came the cataclysmic upheaval in England that both reinforced the apocalyptic expectations of New Englanders and in a few short years reduced their position from that of a city upon a hill to a provincial backwater. It was during this period that missionary work was begun in earnest. By 1647, when it began to be plain that New England would not play a major role in the English rule of saints, there was a steady stream of literature designed both to promote the conversion of the Indians by stressing its historic portentousness and to explain and apologize for the small number of converts to date. What had begun as a secondary consideration suddenly acquired a new significance. If God did not intend the Puritans to return from their wilderness sojourn as the vanguard of world-wide reformation, then He must have sent them into exile so that the uttermost ends of the earth--even the American wilderness--might be prepared for the coming Kingdom. The one great end of God in sending "so many Saints to NEW-ENGLAND" apparently was the regeneration of the Indians. As their friends in England put it, God had planned their persecution and banishment from England "that hee might open a passage for them in the Wildernesse, and make them instruments to draw soules to him who had been so long estranged from him."[22] In 1652 John Endecott could thank God that some had stirred up the Lord among the heathen "which was one end of our comming hither, and it is not frustrated,"[23] while another Puritan declared, "the best News I can write you from New-England is, the Lord is indeed converting the Indians."[24] Increasingly frequent importunities for money and aid from England to succor the missionaries, accompanied with blandishments of imminent

---

[22]"To the Right Honourable the Lords and Commons," signed by Stephen Marshall, Jeremy Whitaker, Edmund Calamy, William Greenhill, John Downam, Philip Nye, Sidrach Simpson, William Carter, Thomas Goodwin, Thomas Case, Simeon Ashe, and Samuel Bolton in Shepard, Clear Sunshine.

[23]Letter in Whitfield, 47.

[24]William French, letter, ibid., 52

success, reached a peak during the 1650's--the time when "many eminent and learned Divines . . . foretold the conversion of the Jewes." The spirit in which these requests were made was epitomized in the question: "If the dawn of the morning be so delightfull, what will the clear day be?"[25]

The colonists' conjecture that the Indians were really Jews--however conducive to bolstering the importance of their errand into the wilderness--turned out to be double-edged. Why, asked their critics, did the coming brighter day continue so long in its dawning stages? There were two grounds for such criticism: first, that the number of conversions was far too small for a colony which had publicly declared its intention to bring the heathen to God; and second, that the conversions made were not genuine. The second criticism was dealt with relatively easily. John Eliot, for instance, published a series of case histories of conversions entitled The Dying Speeches of Several Indians as well as pamphlets setting forth the true power of this pouring out of the Spirit of the Lord in America. Letters and accounts of conversions were published in London as fast as they were written. "The reason wherefore we have published so many testimonialls, and shall insert more, is because too many that come from thence [New England] labour to blast the worke, by reporting here that there is no such worke a foote in the Countrey: or it if be it is but for the loaves, & if any be truely converted, 'tis not above five or seaven at most.'"[26] New Englanders were quick to refute any suggestion that "the charity of the wel-affected hath been abused, in that there is no such work, or that there is a greater noise made of it in the world then there is cause."[27]

The small number of conversions was less easily explained; for if the Puritans were to maintain the reality of the New

---

[25]"To the Right Honourable the Lords and Commons" in Shepard, Clear Sunshine.

[26]Whitfield, 58.

[27]Henry Whitfield, "To the Right Honourable the Parliament of England" in Eliot and Mayhew, The Light Appearing More and More towards the Perfect Day.

England Way, they could not insist on the quantity of converts. To do so would have been in effect to deny the distinction between the visibly regenerate and the rest of mankind. But they had to admit that even if one did measure converts in terms of Praying Indians instead of regenerate Christians, the number of uncivilized and unconverted barbarians was still legion. The problem facing New England apologists was how to emphasize the hopeful beginnings in this work of enlarging Christ's Kingdom and yet account for its slow progress.

Paradoxically, the conversion of the Jews afforded an excellent excuse for their apparent lack of success. Revelation 15 was commonly interpreted to mean that no nation could be converted until the calling of the Jews. Therefore, if one chose to regard the Indians as a Gentile nation instead of western Jews, it was likely, as John Wilson put it, that "till the Jewes come in, there is a seale set upon the hearts of those people, as they thinke from some Apocalypticall places."[28] It was possible to argue that the beginnings of conversion among the Indians should be interpreted apocalyptically while also maintaining that wholesale success could not legitimately be expected until the Jewish nation had become Christian. Thus Wilson, after admitting the possibility that the number of conversions would remain small, could also point out that "what Nation or people ever so deeply degenerated since _Adams_ fall as these Indians, and yet the Spirit of God is working upon them?"[29] In like fashion John Cotton, after encouraging New Englanders with the reminder "To expect the certain Ruine of all false Religions; _Indian_, _Turkish_, yes and _Popish_ too," went on to say that the Indians "are not able, nor shall be able to enter till these Plagues [i.e., those brought on by the pouring out of the seven vials] are fulfilled."[30] In fact, he told

---

[28]_The Day-Breaking, If Not the Sun-Rising of the Gospell with the Indians in New-England_ (London, 1647) 15-16.

[29]_Ibid._, 18.

[30]Quoted in Samuel Sewall, _Phaenomena Quaedam Apocalyptica ad Aspectum Novi Orbis Configurata_ (Boston, 1697), 52. Sewall states that these quotations were taken from Cotton's "Manuscript on _Revelation_."

them, one of the ways in which the inhabitants of New England could best advance the conversion of the Indians was to pray for the calling of the Jews. "If the casting away of the Jews [in the Apostles' time] brought in Asia and Europe (a great part of both) with some part of Africa: How much more shall their Conversion, which is their Fullness, bring in a greater Harvest of these three Parts of the World, and America besides?"[31]

In spite of their apocalyptically hopeful estimate of the possibility of converting the Indians, the Puritans were beginning to have serious doubts about their own ability to overcome the temptations of the wilderness. By the 1640's Winthrop spoke of "wilde beasts and beastlike men" when writing of the wilderness, while Thomas Shepard described it as a place "where we could forecast nothing but care and temptations."[32] "Assuredly the better part of our plantations did undertake the enterprise with a suffering minde . . .," John Eliot explained in 1652, "to go into a wilderness where nothing appeareth but hard labour, wants, and wilderness-temptations."[33] Unquestionably these doubts were partly the result of actual experience of the difficulties of wilderness living. Yet believing as they did that their well-being in the wilderness--both spiritual and physical--depended upon their status as a chosen people, the Puritans could hardly help worrrying about their position in the 1650's. Although the physical wilderness was gradually being pushed back--the colonists could not deny that God had provided them with material sustenance in the New World--the spiritual succor which they had anticipated was not forthcoming. In England the Independents were betraying the cause of congregationalism in the name of tolerance; at home the paucity of regenerate church members seemed to betoken a withdrawal of God's Spirit.

---

[31]Ibid., 52-3.

[32]Shepard and Allin, Massachusetts or the First Planters of New-England, 37.

[33]Quoted in Williams, Church History, 8.

Even the conquest of the physical wilderness was becoming the
occasion for a major wilderness temptation--what Edward Johnson
called "an overweaning desire in most men after Medow-
land."[34] In 1645 Thomas Shepard had been able to assert that
not only were the saints justified in fleeing from England to a
wilderness refuge, but that the Lord had had a great work in
mind "so to carry out a people of his own from so flourishing
State, to a wildernesse so far distant."[35] Shepard was
sure--or at least he endeavored to convince his brethren in
England--that the "fatherly care of our God" in feeding and
clothing so many immigrants, to say nothing of "the form of a
Commonwealth erected in a Wilderness," was proof of the special
providential design behind New England's planting. Nor is it
likely that in 1645 the great work Shepard had in mind was the
conversion of the Indians; more probably it was the creation of
a model church polity. Only six years later Peter Bulkeley
asked, "why hath the Lord brought us hither into this
wilderness, to destroy us?" He answered his question as John
Cotton had predicted such a question would be answered: "But
let us know, it is not the Lord which hath broken promise with
us, but wee have sinned and broken Covenant with him."[36] Two
decades after the founding of the colony, "wilderness-
temptations"--of which the desire for material gain was not the
least--were threatening to overwhelm this outpost of Christ's
Kingdom.

Nevertheless the delicate balance in which the Puritans held
the counterweights of wilderness rewards and temptations had not
yet been irrevocably tipped on the pessimistic side. In 1663 an
enterprising young member of the second generation, Increase
Mather, suggested the possibility that a "wilderness-condition"
per se might possess intrinsic virtue.

---

[34]Johnson, 197.

[35]Shepard and Allin, Massachusetts or the First Planters
of New-England, 37.

[36]Peter Bulkley, The Gospel-Covenant, or The Covenant of
Grace Opened (London, 1653), 300.

> It was an Observation (or an Inspiration rather) of holy
> Brightman's That some faithful ones in a Wilderness should
> have the most clear Discoveries of the Abominations of the
> Man of Sin: which Prophetick passage of that Reverend and
> Learned Writer, some have applied unto those worthy
> Confessors in New-England, who forsook their Country and
> Fathers houses, and left a pleasant Land, farre dearer to
> them then their lives, for the Testimony of Jesus.[37]

When Mather hinted that the wilderness itself offered a godly
people the advantage of unique insight into apocalyptic
mysteries, he was offering his compatriots a way to reconcile
their experience of wilderness trials and temptations and the
difficulties of overcoming them with their expectation of a
special destiny. Instead of being an obstacle to the
fulfillment of their errand in the wilderness--as Peter Bulkeley
had suggested--such trials and temptations were an integral part
of it. Only those tempted and tested in a wilderness were able
to apprehend apocalyptic truths. Had not St. John himself
received the vision recorded in Revelation in a wilderness?

These ideas were developed further by Mather a few years
later in his The Mystery of Israel's Salvation. A treatise on
the predicted conversion of the Jews, this book was a work in
the tradition of Brightman, Forbes, Cotton, and Goodwin.
Mather, however, was more extreme than any of these men in his
apocalyptic views since he like John Davenport was an avowed
chiliast. In this book Mather predicted that the Jews would
soon be restored to Israel and brought to profess Christ by an
extraordinary effusion of God's Spirit. At the same time Rome
and the Turkish empire would fall and the total destruction of
the church's antichristian enemies would begin. This
destruction and the final salvation of the Jews would be
completed shortly thereafter by the appearance of Christ to
begin judgment and inaugurate an age of perfection on earth for
all of the resurrected saints. At the end of a thousand years
(or perhaps more) Christ, having judged all in the world, would

---

[37]Increase Mather, "An Apologetical Preface to the Reader"
in John Davenport, Another Essay for Investigation of the Truth
in Answer to Two Questions (Cambridge, Mass., 1663).

deliver up His mediatory Kingdom to God. Apart from the clearly pre-millennial aspects of Mather's ideas, the most interesting part of this treatise is the section in which he set forth the "uses" of this knowledge for the inhabitants of New England. Mather's main point was that it was important to be acquainted with these truths. "Indeed if these things were cunningly devised fables, or if they were but the uncertain conjectures of men, we might be held excused, though we should not bestow precious time in looking into them; but inasmuch as they are things that shall surely come to pass, the evil will be great if we should not look into these holy Mysteries."[38] New Englanders were especially well qualified to gain knowledge in these apocalyptical matters.

> Some of us are under special advantage to understand these mysterious truths of God; That is to say, such of us are in an exiled condition in this wilderness. Indeed some came hither upon worldly accounts, but others there are that came into this wilderness purely upon spiritual accounts; (yea, and that continue here upon no other account) that so they might bear witness not only against the Name of the Beast, and against his character, but also against his Number . . . h. e. [sic] that so they might bear witness against all humane inventions in the worship of God, who is exceeding jealous as to the manner and means, as well as in respect to the matter of his worship.[39]

Those New Englanders who feared God might expect to be rewarded for their wilderness exile--not with material goods, but with nothing less than knowledge of God's plans for the world. To them the Lord would impart not just the mysteries of grace, but those of divine providence "that they shall know what God is doing, and about to do in the world, though others know nothing of these matters."[40] Consequently such men should bestir themselves to acquire apocalyptic understanding through reading,

---

[38]Mather, The Mystery of Israel's Salvation, 145.

[39]Ibid., 163.

[40]Ibid., 169.

130

meditation, earnest prayer, and godly discourse. "And truly, if
they that fear God when they meet together, instead of worldly
discourse, . . . would speak one to another in a serious manner
concerning the glorious kingdom of Christ, in the day when he
shall restore the kingdom unto Israel, it would be much more for
their comfort in the day of accounts."[41]

In this way Mather set forth his answer to Bulkeley's
question. The Lord had dispatched His people to this savage and
faraway country not just to find a place of refuge nor just to
reap the material benefits of a promised land. He had sent them
because certain truths necessary for the advance of history
could be learned only in a wilderness exile. For Mather the
wilderness had acquired an additional meaning to those it had
had for the first generation--a meaning which enabled him to
maintain that the colonists were a chosen people in spite of the
fact that they had been unable to convert the wilderness into a
spiritual garden of the Lord. "God hath led us into a
wilderness, and surely it was not because the Lord hated us, but
because he loved us, that he brought us hither into this
Jeshimon [a biblical synonym for wilderness]. Who knoweth but
that he may send down his spirit upon us here, if we continue
faithful before him?"[42]

Mather was unable wholly to exorcise fears (including his
own) that New England was doomed to remain a spiritual
wilderness. But for a while there was at least as much evidence
to support his claim that the colonists had been sent into the
wilderness because God loved them as there was to support the
opposite contention. By the time The Mystery of Israel's
Salvation was published in 1669, Boston had ceased to be a
frontier outpost and could have been compared with most
provincial cities in England. Unfriendly Indians were held in

---

[41]Ibid., 170.

[42]Ibid., 164.

check by various treaties. There had been no outbreak of
hostility since the colonists had decisively defeated the
Pequots in 1637. Occasional war scares did not allow New
Englanders to forget that unconverted Indians represented an
ever-present threat, but settlements had expanded as far west as
Deerfield and relations with the Indians remained peaceful.
Missionary work showed encouraging, if not apocalyptic, signs of
growth. (In 1674 there were fourteen villages of Praying
Indians in Massachusetts alone.) In spite of the lamentations
of local jeremiahs over the decay of godliness and their threats
of divine punishment, New England had survived the Restoration
without suffering a serious political disaster. Even the
passage of the Navigation Acts had failed to impair the
country's burgeoning prosperity. Into this relatively placid
atmosphere, the great Indian uprising known as King Philip's War
erupted like a withering blast of wrath from God. This
catastrophe--which was close to being what the twentieth century
calls "total war"--was a sudden and rude confirmation of the
Puritans' doubts about the wilderness. Overnight the Indians
ceased to be regarded as potential converts and became stealthy
and treacherous beasts of prey, utilizing the cover of a vast
and hideous wilderness to attack their would-be benefactors.
The possibility of regarding the wilderness as a promised land
or a place of refuge was submerged--although not destroyed--by
this concrete evidence of its savage nature.

Naturally New Englanders interpreted the war as a divine
warning that God was about to uproot His faithless
"plantation." When the outbreak of the war was followed by
extensive fires in Boston, epidemics of smallpox, and increasing
hostility on the part of the Stuart government, Massachusetts
ministers decided that there was need of "a more full enquiry
into the Causes & State of Gods Controversy with us."[43] The
Reforming Synod of 1679 was called to determine "What are the
euills that haue provoked the Lord to bring his judgments on New
England?" and "What is to be donn that so those euills may be
reformed?"[44] The answers of the Reforming Synod to these

---

[43]Petition to General Court, May 28, 1679, in Walker, 414.

[44]Vote of General Court on Petition in Walker, 416.

questions were far from novel. In the established pattern of
the jeremiads, the congregated ministers set forth the special
status of New England in the eyes of the Lord, who had been
pleased to show those exiled in the wilderness "the Pattern of
his House, and all the forms there." Recounting the "most
peculiar mercies and privileges" He had bestowed upon "this his
People," the ministers went on to enumerate the provoking sins
of the land--first and foremost of which was "a great and
visible decay of the power of Godliness amongst many Professors
in these Churches."[45] They then proceeded to the remedies at
hand, particularly enjoining churches to a "Solemn and explicit
Renewal of the Covenant."

It was by no means clear that the Reforming Synod had much
confidence in the enduring efficacy of the reforms which they
were advocating. The ministers had been stressing the need for
reformation for at least twenty-five years without any marked
increase in visible godliness. Neither threats of hell-fire nor
appeals to the colonists' sense of communal responsibility had
sufficed to bring about that measure of holiness so essential to
the well-being of God's people in the wilderness. It is not
surprising, therefore, to discover that the very last
recommendation in the Synod's list was an injunction to pray for
an outpouring of the Lord's Spirit as the only truly efficacious
means of restoring New England's godliness.

Inasmuch as a thorough and heart Reformation is necessary,
in order to obtaining peace with God, Jer. 3. 10. and all
outward means will be ineffectual unto that end, except the
Lord pour down his Spirit from on High, it doth therefore
concern us to cry mightily unto God, both in ordinary and
extraordinary manner, that he would be pleased to rain down
Righteousness upon us.[46]

The Synod's recommendation that New Englanders "cry mightily
unto God" for righteousness constituted an official admission of
the colonists' inability to complete the errand undertaken by

---

[45]Result of the Synod of 1679 in Walker, 427.

[46]Ibid., 437.

their fathers. Like Samuel Hooker, who two years earlier had
recognized "the utter insufficiency of all means in themselves
considered," the Synod had been forced back upon an essentially
apocalyptic solution to New England's problems--an outpouring of
the Spirit.

It was not until the 1690's that the apocalyptic
implications behind the Synod's recommendation were made fully
explicit. By then it was apparent that the Reforming Synod had
been completely unsuccessful in coping with the problem of
declension. Not only had New Englanders failed to become more
godly, they were rent with dissension and subjected to disaster
after disaster. During the closing years of the seventeenth
century the colonists had lost their charter, suffered under
Andros, undertaken two disasterous attempts to capture Quebec,
fought the Indians, and last, but not least, endured the tragedy
of the witchcraft trials. It is no wonder then that New England
experienced a resurgence of millennial thinking comparable to
that of the 1640's and the early 1650's. This time, however,
such thinking was limited to a relatively small, but very
influential group of clergymen ministering in and near Boston.
Including Cotton and Increase Mather, John Higginson, Nicholas
Noyes, Samuel Willard, and a layman, Samuel Sewall, this group
sought to save the New England Way from its threatened
dissolution by revitalizing the apocalyptic expectations of the
first generation. Inevitably the experience of wilderness
living--the fact that all of these men had spent the greater
part of their lives in the New World--influenced their thought.
For these men the wilderness setting of the New England Way had
become an essential part of it.

Perhaps the man who expressed this attitude best was Judge
Samuel Sewall. Like Edward Johnson, another layman, Sewall was
among the most ardent exponents of the apocalyptic possibilities
of the New World. In a treatise on apocalyptic prophecies
published in 1697, (_Phaenomena Quaedem Apocalyptica_), he set out
to prove that America would be the site of New Jerusalem in the
coming millennium. Interestingly enough, the immediate occasion
for the composition of this work seems to have been Sewall's
desire to refute aspersions cast on New England over sixty years
earlier by Joseph Mede. Sewall apparently owned a one-volume
edition of Mede's works published in 1672 which contained a

large number of letters on millennial topics. Among the letters
printed in this collection were several from William Twisse, a
prominent Presbyterian divine during the Interregnum, who had
been converted by Mede to his millennarian ideas. In 1634
Twisse wrote to Mede asking his opinion of the English
plantations in the New World. His curiosity about them had been
aroused, he told Mede, by the contemplation of God's providence
in withholding discovery of America until so near the end of the
world. Considering the widely held belief that the Gospel would
flee westward, Twisse wanted to know "why may not that be the
place of New Jerusalem?" This was a somewhat rhetorical
question, since Mede had already convinced Twisse that New
Jerusalem would be in Israel. Nevertheless, Twisse was anxious
to know what would happen to the English in America.

> But what? I pray, shall our _English_ there degenerate and
> joyn themselves with Gog and Magog? We have heard lately
> divers ways, that our people there have no hope of the
> Conversion of the Natives. And the very week after I
> received your last Letter, I saw a Letter written from New
> England, discoursing of an impossibility of subsisting
> there; and seems to prefer the confession of God's Truth in
> any condition here in Old England, rather than run over to
> enjoy their liberty there.[47]

Mede's reply confirmed Twisse's worst fears about the New
World. After professing that he wished the colonists as well as
anybody--"though I differ from them far, both in other things,
and in the grounds they go upon"[48]--Mede set forth his
conviction that America and its native inhabitants were
peculiarly the domain of Satan. According to him, the Devil had
lured "some of those barbarous Nations dwelling upon the
Northern Ocean" over into America at the time of Christ's first
coming in order to preserve himself a kingdom. In spite of the
presence of Christian men among them, there was little, if any,
hope for their conversion. As for the English who had so
bravely invaded Satan's kingdom, the best Mede could hope for

---

[47]_The Works of . . . Joseph Mede_, 799.

[48]_Ibid._

them was that "they shall not so far degenerate (not all of
them) as to come in that Army of <u>Gog</u> and <u>Magog</u> against the
Kingdom of Christ."[49]

Samuel Sewall's reaction to these aspersions upon New
England was unequivocally patriotic. That indeed is the most
appropriate word with which to describe his book. His avowed
motive was "to expose this Antick Fancy of America's being
Hell."[50] "Wherefore, I hope our honoured Mother will not
account it undutifull or indecent for me to say, The Inhabitants
of <u>Boston</u> in <u>Lincoln-shire</u> are no less <u>Inferi</u> [sic] to us; than
the Inhabitants of <u>Boston</u> in <u>New-England</u> are to them."[51] To
prove the equality, if not the superiority of New to Old
England, Sewall was prepared to convert all of its apparent
"wilderness" liabilities into assets. For instance, although he
could not deny that the conversion of the Indians had not lately
been proceeding as well as it should have, he denied that this
meant they were permanently enslaved to the Devil.

> The sorrowful Decay and Languishing of the Work in many
> places, since that time [i.e., the first years of the
> colony]; and the little faith that is to be found in
> exercise concerning it: are so far from being a ground of
> Discouragement; that it gives us cause to expect that the
> set Time draweth very near for our blessed Lord Jesus Christ
> to be Recognized and Crowned KING of Kings; and LORD of
> Lords. And I humbly crave leave to enter a Claim, that the
> New World may be no longer made an Outcast: but may be
> admitted to assist at the CORONATION.[52]

According to Sewall, the idea that Christ would desert "what He
hath already got in <u>New England</u>", was far less probable than

---

[49]<u>Ibid.</u>, 800.

[50]Sewall, 39.

[51]<u>Ibid.</u>, 40.

[52]<u>Ibid.</u>, "To the Honorable William Stoughton."

that He would soon bring on a glorious reformation in New
Spain. Sewall asserted that Christ could not come "till the
Indians be Gospellized," and exhorted his compatriots to do all
they could to bring this about.[53] He took the battle into the
opposite camp by linking Mede's famous Clavis Apocalypticae with
the founding of New England. It was "not altogether
inconsiderable" that Mede's commentary on Revelation "which was
a notable means to revive the Thinking and Speaking of New
Jerusalem"--was first published in 1627, since that same year
"the Design for planting of the Gospel in New England, began to
be ripened."[54] In 1628, Sewall reminded his readers, the first
town in Massachusetts Bay was begun and was called Salem, "which
may give occasion to hope, that GOD intendeth to write upon
these Churches the Name of New Jerusalem: They shall be near of
Kin to, and shall much resemble that City of GOD."[55] Sewall's
faith that the churches of his land would ultimately "much
resemble" New Jerusalem--in spite of their declensions--was
essentially a reaffirmation of the apocalyptic spirit in which
the first generation had created the New England Way. But
clearly for Sewall the wilderness into which the first colonists
had been sent was more important than the errand on which they
had been dispatched. He defended New England's destiny, not so
much because it was vitally important for history's consummation
as simply because it was New England's.

Sewall's patriotic interpretation of apocalyptic mysteries
was echoed a year later in an election sermon preached by
Nicolas Noyes. Noyes' topic in this sermon was the declension
of New England. Although he too lamented the decay of
godliness, he went to great pains to make it clear that this
decay was in no way an inevitable concomitant of the American
environment. If New England had declined, it had become no more
degenerate than the rest of the Protestant world. If Antichrist
(in the person of the Spaniard) had taken possession of the New

---

[53]Ibid., 55.

[54]Ibid., 51.

[55]Ibid.

World when the Reformation drove him from the Old, Christ had "followed him at the heels and [taken] Possession of America for Himself. And this Province, so far as I know, is the very Turf and Twig He took Possession by; as to the Reformation and Conversion of the Natives, and gathering of them into Churches."[56] If some had conjectured that America might be headquarters for Gog and Magog, or even "Hell it self," others had suggested that it might be the New Jerusalem. The New World was no worse off morally or spiritually than the Old and certainly had an equal claim to any apocalyptic bounty of the Spirit which might be forthcoming. "Now as for New England, if the First Planters of it had dream'd that the very Situation of Climate of the Land had been crime enough to make men aliens from the Covenants of promise; they would not have Sold their European Birthright, for a mess of American Pottage. For ought I can see to the contrary, our Declensions are the worst Omen and Objection against us; and Reformation would be the best Answer to them: and Hope and Prayer are powerful helps and inducements to it."[57]

When Noyes recommended hope and prayer as the best means to bring about New England's reformation, he was thinking in apocalyptic terms. In the same sermon he encouraged "all good people to hope and pray for the Restaurations, Reformations, and Divine Benedictions promised to Jews, or Christians; or prophesied to come to them in the latter days; and [to pray] that we in New England may through the Grace of God, have a share in the good things spoken of."[58] God's promises of apocalyptic blessing for His people applied not only to the Jews, but to "Christian places that are in ruines, over-run with sin & misery." Thus--and this was the essence of Noyes' message--New Englanders did not have to rely upon their own efforts to achieve the reformation so necessary to the country's well-being. "Many speak as if only the Restauration and

---

[56]Nicholas Noyes, New Englands Duty and Interest to Be a Habitation of Justice and Mountain of Holiness (Boston, 1698), 75.

[57]Ibid., 76.

[58]Ibid., 60.

Benediction were promised; and look upon Reformation as the
condition of the Promise. And because they see not the
condition fulfilled; cannot believe the Restaurations &
Blessings."[59] New England's reformation depended "upon the
good pleasure of God," and what God had promised, He would not
deny. "If the Restaurations depended on the <u>Antecedency</u> of
Reformation, and Reformation depended upon man's <u>free will</u>, it
would be long enough before either would come to pass. But God
having foretold & promised both, our dependence ought to be on
his <u>Grace</u> and <u>Truth</u> and <u>Power</u>."[60] When the foreordained time
of reformation did come, God would cause the "<u>Rain of
Righteousness</u>" to fall upon the just and the unjust alike. Then
"bad men" would become good, and "good men" would become
better. The colonists had no reason to fear for their country's
destiny. "Notwithstanding the present bad circumstances of
<u>America</u>, I know no reason to conclude this Continent shall not
partake of <u>the Goodness of God in the latter days</u>."[61]

Two years after Noyes' sermon was published, Samuel Willard
reiterated his hopeful message in a classic exposition of New
England millennial thought. "<u>There are happy Times predicted for
the Church</u>," he wrote, "<u>after her wilderness estate shall be
over</u>."[62] Just as Israel passed through a wilderness before
entering Canaan, so the church militant--as predicted in
Revelation--had to spend 1260 "days" in the wilderness, after
which "God hath promised to it in this world, a more glorious
Conspicuous state."[63] Willard was sure that these happy times
were very close. Men should look for a "transcendently greater
Glory" than any which had gone before "making hast to appear."
This glory would coincide with the calling of the Jews, the

---

[59]<u>Ibid.</u>, 61.

[60]<u>Ibid.</u>, 63.

[61]<u>Ibid.</u>, 68-9.

[62]Samuel Willard, <u>The Fountain Opened</u> (Boston, 1700), 114.

[63]<u>Ibid.</u>,

the fullness of the Gentiles, and the destruction of Antichrist, all of which were to be accomplished by God's "giving an enlarged Commission for the Preaching of the Everlasting Gospel."[64] Satan would be bound and the world would enjoy an access of spiritual felicity. "The great glory of these times will be, that Grace will then flourish, and holiness abound."[65] Willard was careful to point out that since this period of felicity would be enjoyed by the church militant and not by the church triumphant (whose glory would come after the Last Judgment), it would be a happiness "not of absolute, but comparative perfection." Unlike the Mathers, whose chiliasm postulated a period of absolute perfection for the church on earth, Willard did not depart from the more conservative views which had been held by John Cotton and Thomas Goodwin, Willard openly rebuked the extremism typical of the Mathers. "The visible Church it self is a mixt company, and it is so like to continue till the end of the world, when a separation is to be made."[66] Hence men should learn "the vanity" of those who expected absolute perfection before the end. "To think on a day on this side of Eternal Glory, or during the Evangelical Dispensation of the Kingdom of Christ, in which there shall be neither ignorance, nor error, nor trouble upon the professing people of God, is but to dream: and those who feed themselves up with such a hope, do but feed on ashes. It is true, there is a time that will come ere long, wherein the priviledges of the Church both spiritual and temporal shall be great to admiration, but still it will have a mixture of darkness in it."[67]

---

[64]Ibid., 116.

[65]Ibid., 117.

[66]Samuel Willard, The Checkered State of the Gospel Church (Boston, 1701), 20.

[67]Ibid., 21-2.

The conclusions Willard drew from these ideas concerning the prospects for New England were optimistic. The colonists could anticipate an immediate benefit from these expected happy times, "inasmuch as it is rationally to be supposed that this light will have its gradual increase, & not attain to its Meridian at once, as the darkness into which the Church went in its retirement into the wilderness, was gradual."[68] If this were so, then no matter how far New England had declined nor how great was its decay in godliness, there was still reason to hope that God would revive the country with an effusion of His Spirit. It was, Willard reminded his congregation, darkest just before the dawn.

By the end of the seventeenth century God's "plantation" in New England was firmly rooted. Notwithstanding its current difficulties, New England was a land which God had "Signally owned & blessed," particularly in terms of material benefits. It was also true that God's people had not answered either "the Lords Expectation, or our own Profession." Clearly the inhabitants of New England had an obligation to fulfill, and in "the latter dayes" which were rapidly bringing the world to its end, there was ample reason to expect that they would be provided with the spiritual wherewithal to fulfill it. As John Higginson, one of the colony's oldest ministers, put it: "It is without question the duty of the Church and People of God to be an Habitation of Justice and Mountain of Holiness, . . . and because God hath foretold and promised that it shall be Eminently & Conspicuously so at some times and in some places in these last dayes that are come and coming upon the World, therefore we are to aime at it and endeavour after it, . . . for it is certain, so far as we attain thereunto we shall be a People blessed of the Lord."[69]

---

[68]Ibid., 53-4.

[69]"The Epistle Dedicatory" in Noyes.

Chapter VI.

SOLOMON STODDARD

For all the equivocations and ambiguities of the Halfway
Covenant, the first great rent in the fabric of the federal
theology was Solomon Stoddard's denial of the church covenant.
In 1677 Stoddard, minister of frontier Northampton and later the
powerful "pope" of the Connecticut River Valley, opened the
Lord's Supper to virtually the entire town, making no attempt to
distinguish between the regenerate and the unregenerate. To the
chagrin of Bostonian keepers of orthodoxy, he followed this
heresy two years later with a "revival of the power of
godliness" such as they had long been praying for. Altogether
in his long career, Stoddard reaped five harvests of souls, and
his success where the guardians of the New England Way were
conspicuously lacking was so much salt rubbed in the wound of
ruptured unity. With Stoddard the "unity of spirit" which
Winthrop had propounded as the first requirement of a
New-England Israel was irrevocably shattered. In spite of
Matherian pretenses to the contrary, New England henceforth
could no longer claim to be "knitt together in this worke as one
man."

Stoddard's justification for thus robbing New England of its
putative glory was simply that he found no Scriptural grounds
for the church covenant. "There is," he said "no Syllable in
the Word of God, intimating any such thing, neither is there any
need of it."[1] The bounds of the church should be determined
by agreement or authority, "but there is no occasion that every
Member should Covenant particularly with the Church."[2] If
there were no church covenant, there was no necessity for
distinguishing between saints and sinners. Such distinctions
had a tendency "to nourish carnal confidence in them that are
admitted [to the Lord's Supper], and to nourish prophaneness in
them that are excluded."[3] Stoddard denied that there were any

---

[1]The Doctrine of Instituted Churches Explained and Proved
from the Word of God (London, 1700), 8.

[2]Ibid.

[3]Solomon Stoddard, The Inexcusableness of Neglecting the
Worship of God (Boston, 1708), 20.

objective standards by which one man could judge the regeneracy
of another: "No man can look into the heart of another, and see
the workings of a gracious Spirit."[4]   If God had intended a
distinction between the elect and the damned, He would have
provided some unmistakable sign by which they could be
discerned. On these grounds Stoddard administered the Lord's
Supper to all those not openly scandalous who made a profession
of faith, and he persistently refused to require evidence of an
"experimental" conversion.

The power behind this summary rejection of the New England
Way derived from Stoddard's conception of God--His absolute
power, His unconditioned will, His incomprehensible love and
mercy. In his first book, The Safety of Appearing at the Day of
Judgment in the Righteousness of Christ, his concern was to
reassure men of the efficacy of Christ's mediation between
sinful man and this glorious Being. Confronted with the
awfulness of a God whose "Sovereign Will and Pleasure" alone
were "Sufficient to move him to choose one and refuse another,"
men could be comforted by the knowledge God had covenanted
Himself to act in accordance with the law revealed in His Word.
"God has stated the Law to be a rule of proceeding towards man:
wherein he has set down the terms upon which he will bestow life
and execute death; in that covenant, he gave not onely a Law
unto man, but likewise to himself, from which he will never
swerve."[5]   Having bound both Himself and His creatures to the
observance of the Law, God had then in His mercy sent Christ to
fulfill its requirement of perfect righteousness--a requirement
which no man after the Fall would have been able to fulfill.
The assurance of the believer, therefore, was that of a man who
has contracted and then fulfilled his contract: "The heart will
not be satisfied in the safety of coming to Christ, except he
see a way how the Law is answered . . . he that understands not
the strictness of the Law cannot see the need of Christ, and he

---

[4]The Falseness of the Hopes of Many Professors (Boston,
1708), 11.

[5]Solomon Stoddard, The Safety of Appearing at the Day of
Judgment in the Righteousness of Christ (Boston, 1687), 24.

that understands not the sufferings of Christ cannot see the safety that is in Christ."[6]

All of this differed not a whit from orthodox federal theology. The real difference bewteen Stoddard and his contemporaries lay in his insistence that the workings of God's will were so far beyond the understandings of men that no intelligible prediction concerning them could be made. God chose as He willed; those whom He chose believed; these He had promised to save. To predicate a society upon the knowledge of these unknowable determinations--as had New England's founders--was blasphemous. No human covenant, be it that of church or nation, no conditioning factor whatsoever extended to that original act of divine will. "The only reason why God sets his love on one man and not upon another is, because he pleases: he acts the soveraignty of his own will in it; it is his own will that makes the difference between men."[7] Precisely because no one could fathom the profundities of that free will--"how can the light of nature reach the free determination of the Will of God?"[8]--in human society everyone had an equal opportunity to be saved. This or that particular man was as capable of being loved by God as any other in the World. It was true that "the children of godly Parents" with whom God was striving by his Spirit were "more likely than others, but one is as capable as the other; for the free will of God is the only thing that does determine it: and therefore you have sufficient ground of encouragement to accept the offer of salvation."[9]

Because God's will could not be conditioned, every man had an equally probable claim in this world to be a member of the elect and hence an equal right to the sacraments. Those who were privileged to live "under means," even the means available in a reformed land, were at best only _more_ likely to be

---

[6] _Ibid._, 98.

[7] _Ibid._, 325.

[8] _Ibid._, 3.

[9] _Ibid._, 327.

converted. They could not be certain of it. The considerations
of this world had no existence in the determination of God's
will. Among these had to be numbered a heritage of
righteousness and membership in a chosen community. Men would
stand or fall at Judgment Day on evidence of their belief in
Christ--not upon their citizenship in this world.

Stoddard, examining the founders' city upon a hill in the
light of his understanding of God's unconditioned will, came to
the conclusion that Massachusetts could lay no claim to a
special status in the eyes either of God or of the world. Here
lay the essence of his protest against the ancestor-
oriented insistence of the Mathers and their colleagues upon a
congregational policy. Stoddard rejected the conception of a
New-English Israel as incompatible with God's liberty. He
remained utterly unconvinced that New England had an apocalyptic
destiny and hence found no reason in Scripture or the light of
nature for maintaining a polity that fostered "carnal
confidence" and "prophaneness." As far as he was concerned, the
Reformation had not reached its climax in "primitive"
congregationalism. "If the practises of our Fathers in any
particulars were mistakes, it is fit they should be rejected, if
they be not, they will bear Examination: If we be forbidden to
Examine their practices, that will cut off all hopes of
Reformation."[10] The most pressing problem of New England was
not the maintenance of accomplished reformation until the end of
time, but a continuous searching after the truth and a
willingness to accept further reform.

Stoddard's abrogation of the church covenant on these
neo-Calvinist grounds predictably pushed the Mathers to even
greater excesses of ancestor worship. For them Stoddard's
innovation involved much more than mere disrespect for the
founders. To men accustomed to viewing the preservation of the
congregational polity as a sacred (in the fullest sense of the
word) trust from which they would be released only by death or
Judgment Day, it opened up all the terrifying possibilities
inherent in a loss of destiny and identity. It is not
surprising that in the years following Stoddard's defection

---

[10]Stoddard, The Inexcusableness of Neglecting the Worship
of God, "Preface."

their lamentations over New England's decline from the ideals of its founders were increasingly coupled with chiliastic predictions of the end of the world. Exploiting to the fullest the earlier trend toward hellfire preaching, the Mathers underlined these threats with hopes either that the Last Judgment would arrive in time to snatch New England's apocalyptic glory from the hands of its malefactors, or that minute descriptions of the horrors of hell would magically produce a revival of godliness. No one knew better than the Mathers that "the Congregational Church Discipline, is not suited for Worldly Interest, or for a Formal Generation of Professors. It will stand or fall as Godliness in the Power of it does prevail or otherwise. That there is a great decay of the Power of Religion throughout all New England is Lamentably true. If that revive, there will be not fear of Departing from the Holy Discipline of the Churches of Christ."[11]

After Increase's admission in 1686 that hellfire preaching produced conversions, Cotton keynoted the decade of the 1690's in a sermon prophetically entitled Things to Be Looked for. The gist of this publication was the proximity of that "wonderful STATE of External PEACE, which the God of Heaven will make His People upon Earth, to be the Joyful Partakers of."[12] When he had described this chiliastic millennium in detail, Mather justified his predictions by setting forth the most recent "Signs of the times," which included the defeat of the Turks and William III's appearance as Protestantism's champion against Antichrist. Just a year later, he prefaced Samuel Lee's Great Day of Judgment with mathematical calculations of hell's infinity and promptly progressed from the object to the lesson in A Midnight Cry: "We ought so to behave our selves as if our Lord were immediately to break in upon the World: and call us before His Great and High Tribunal, to give an Account of what

---

[11]Increase Mather, The Order of the Gospel (Boston, 1700), 11.

[12]Cotton Mather, Things to Be Looked for (Boston, 1691), 7.

we have been <u>doing in the Body</u>."[13] Doubtless, he continued,
we are very near the last hours of the world. New Englanders,
therefore, should renew and "fulfill" their baptismal covenants.

The climax of these efforts (if one excludes the <u>Magnalia</u>)
to save New England from itself and its enemies--in addition to
Stoddard, the Mathers had to deal with witches, Whitehall, and
the insurrection of Brattle Street--came in 1698 with Cotton's
<u>Eleutheria, Or an Idea of the Reformation in England</u>. Opening
with the statement that "we have seen a <u>great</u> REVOLUTION, and we
are e're long to see a <u>greater</u>," Mather set himself to answer
the "considerable questions" which he presumed were then
troubling the minds of Englishmen. In this task "there can
scarce any more significant thing be offered, than an
incontestible <u>Idea</u> and <u>History</u> of the REFORMATION."[14] Firm in
his faith that the problems of Old as well as New England could
be solved by a right apprehension of the true course of history,
Cotton once again plotted the trajectory of reformation from the
first apostasy of Rome to the errand into the wilderness. "But
is [it] not here enough to anticipate the Apprehensions of my
Reader, that the truest and furthest [sic] Recovery out of the
<u>Romish Apostasy</u> hitherto seen, is that which they that go by the
Name of <u>Non-Conformists</u> in the <u>English</u> <u>Nation</u>, have
endeavoured? And that it is not possible for the Church to
recover effectually out of this <u>Apostacy</u>, without acting upon
such <u>Principles</u> as we have at last produced in the <u>American</u>
Desarts, a whole Nation of <u>Non-Conformists</u>?"[15] Irresistibly,
inevitably, the fulfillment of history was bringing cosmic
justification of New England's existence: "<u>Lift up your heads</u>
ye Reforming Churches of God, <u>because Redemption draweth nigh</u>.
The <u>Hundred and four-score</u> years are almost out; and then an
irresistible Spirit of REFORMATION showred from the Lord Jesus

---

[13]Cotton Mather, <u>A Midnight Cry</u> (Boston, 1692), 22.

[14]Cotton Mather, <u>Eleutheria, Or, an Idea of the
Reformation in England</u> (London, 1698), 3.

[15]<u>Ibid.</u>, 27.

Christ on the Hearts of men, shall bring mighty and happy
Changes upon the World."[16]

For the Mathers and their "orthodox" colleagues, the decade
of the 1690's produced a state of affairs in New England that
could only be regarded as incipient chaos. In the midst of
disintegration the most hopeful, indeed for them the only,
interpretation of such a condition was that God was about to
complete history with the full complement of horrendous
happenings foretold in Revelation. The necessity of maintaining
at least the appearance of unity prevented Cotton and Increase
from replying directly to Stoddard before the opening of the
eighteenth century. But in the closing years of the Puritan
century, their extremes of chiliastic fervor, as well as the
sustained fortissimo of their jeremiads, may be read as indirect
refutations of the aspersions which Stoddard had cast upon New
England's destiny. The whole significance of Stoddard's revolt
and the Mather's reaction to it is neatly contained in
Increase's lament: "Would he bring the Churches in New-England
back to the Imperfect Reformation in other Lands, and so deprive
us of our Glory forever?"[17]

Stoddard's fundamental disagreement with the tenets of
Congregational orthodoxy was even more clearly set forth in his
The Doctrine of Instituted Churches, published in 1700. The
Mathers had "anticipated" it with Increase's The Order of the
Gospel and with this thrust and riposte the controversy came
squarely into the open. At its heart lay the idea of the
national covenant. Both Stoddard and the Mathers believed in
the national covenant and urged its obligations upon the
colonists; but their conceptions of it not only differed, but
were contradictory. The Mathers were heir to the conception of
the national covenant which had developed after the introduction
of the requirement of visible regeneration for church
membership. They regarded it as the commitment of a political
entity to a unique obligation; namely, the preservation of
purity in ordinances, people, and churches until the coming of
Judgment. The national covenant in their eyes was the casing

[16]Ibid., 87.

[17]Quoted in Miller, From Colony to Province, 286.

which had been specially manufactured by God to house His truth during the turmoil of the world's disintegration. In this sense it functioned as a substitute for a national church--an antichristiancorruption--during the penultimate phases of history. By binding the political community in a divine covenant complete with sanctions of providential reward and punishment, the founders had succeeded in committing a formally independent magistracy to governing in the interests of religious purity and unity--thus proving to themselves and the world that church purity and independence were compatible with civil government. Up to the loss of the charter, Massachusetts Bay Colony could have been described as a theocracy, not because the civil power was subject to the clergy, but because--theoretically at least--the magistracy itself was actively, expressly and paramountly dedicated to the maintenance of God's truth. By means of the national covenant, New England had achieved all the stability and uniformity that a national church could offer without sacrificing the quintessence of purity that was the gathered church. In the eyes of the Mathers this was the achievement upon which the colonists necessarily had to base their claim to be a chosen people.

Stoddard, on the other hand, would not admit that New England's claim to be a people of God rested on such a narrow base. To him the national covenant was a synonym rather than a substitute for a national church. "What is a National Church but a Professing Nation jointly bound to keep Covenant with God."[18] As far as he was concerned, the maintenance of a covenantal relationship between God and New England depended not upon the number of visibly regenerate members in the churches, but simply upon righteousness of the people as a whole. By this definition of the national covenant, any Christian people could be bound to keep faith with God. They need not be a nation with a unique mission--a people chosen, for instance, to exemplify the purity of regenerate church order until the advent of the millennium. Stoddard, in fact, could see no opposition between churches being national and congregational. "A Nation that is in Covenant with God is a National Church, a Nation that are in

---

[18]Solomon Stoddard, <u>An Appeal to the Learned</u> (Boston, 1709), 55.

Covenant with God are the People of God, bound jointly and severally to keep Covenant with him. God is one party in the Covenant, and they are the other, and being bound together tokeep Covenant, the whole must have power over the parts, to rectify all Mal-administrations, and to see the Covenant kept."[19] The purpose of the national covenant in Stoddard's eyes was simply the reward of good and the punishment of evil--not, as the Mathers stubbornly maintained, the preservation of the New England Way. "This is the Covenant of God, that Holiness shall be rewarded, and Sin shall be punished."[20] Only in these terms did the idea of a national covenant make sense; for a people could be bound to perform only what they were capable of doing, no more and no less than external righteousness: "The visible people of God are able to keep the external Covenant."[21] Being a citizen of New England entailed per se no more than the lawful performance of instituted worship and moral duties; it did not--as the Mathers implied--place one under the obligation to become sanctified. "Sanctifying Grace is necessary unto the right discharge of moral duties, as well as instituted: but it is not necessary unto the lawful attending of Moral duties, or the lawful attending of Instituted duties; and as men may not excuse themselves from moral duties from the want of Grace, so they may not excuse themselves from any duty of Worship."[22]

Stoddard perceived what the Mathers would not admit, or rather could admit only at the cost of their conception of New England's special destiny; namely, that to make the national covenant dependent upon the maintenance of the church covenant was either implicitly to bind God to the sanctification of large numbers of the community or to make demands of unregenerate men

---

[19]Ibid.

[20]Solomon Stoddard, The Danger of Speedy Degeneracy Held Forth in a Sermon Preached at the Lecture in Boston (Boston, 1705), 21.

[21]Stoddard, An Appeal to the Learned, 84.

[22]Stoddard, The Inexcusableness of Neglecting the Worship of God, 3.

which they by definition were incapable of fulfilling. Neither
interpretation would square with Stoddard's conception of God as
an inconceivably omnipotent Being whose "sovereign Will and
Pleasure" could not be fathomed nor whose merciful love could be
measured. "There is a consistency in Gods command: He does not
lay a tye upon mens Consciences to come, and lay a tye upon
their Consciences to forbear; God makes them promise to keep his
Covenant; and will he make it criminal to attend those duties of
the Covenant, which he has made them promise to keep?"[23] It
was simply nonsense to argue as Increase Mather that "altho' it
is true that if a man does know that he is not a Saint, but in a
State of Sin, he ought not to come [to the Lord's Supper]; it
does not follow that a real Saint should neglect coming,
because, he wants Assurance."[24] This made a mockery of divine
justice. From beginning to end, Stoddard's case against federal
orthodoxy rested upon the conviction that "the Lord is a
righteous God, and would never punish men for not believing if
they had not abundant encouragement to believe."[25] On these
terms Stoddard too was prepared to admit with the Mathers that
New England had declined--not from the unparalleled heights of
an apocalyptic destiny, but rather from the less pretentious
heights of simple godliness.

In the years that followed Stoddard's controversy with the
Mathers, his conception of the national covenant gained an
increasing number of adherents among New England clergymen. For
he himself was incontrovertible proof that New England occupied
no unique place in God's regard. He had abrogated the church
covenant; he had denied that the community as a whole was bound
by extraordinary requirements of righteousness. Yet God blessed
his ministry with not one but five outpourings of the Spirit.
Stoddard proved to his own and many others' satisfaction that
God would dispense His Spirit whether or not New Englanders kept

---

[23]Stoddard, An Appeal to the Learned, 83.

[24]Increase Mather, A Dissertation Wherein the Strange
Doctrine Lately Published in a Sermon . . . is Examined and
Confuted (Boston, 1708), 84.

[25]Stoddard, The Safety of Appearing, 110.

the faith of their fathers with Him. This was the indisputable, unavoidable, and infuriating fact the Mathers could not get around, no matter how hard they tried. Eventually it defeated them. If New England clergymen were really interested in the salvation of men's souls--and they could hardly claim otherwise--then they could not afford to ignore the evidence of Stoddard's success nor long refuse to emulate the means by which he achieved it. Their gradual recognition of this fact constituted an important contribution to a developing tradition of revivalism.

In 1702 Increase Mather, bedevilled beyond endurance by his opponents, was driven so far as to confess "that which some have thought was the special design of Providence in bringing a choice People into this part of the world, seems as if it were now over. It has been by Good and Wise men conjectured, that the Lords more peculiar design in Planting these Heavens and Laying the Foundation of this Earth, was, that the world might see a Specimen of what shall be over all the Earth in the Glorious Times which are Expected, . . . It was very much thus in New England many years ago. But neither our Civil or Ecclesiastical State is ever like to be what once it was."[26] As one might expect, Mather's assertion that the errand into the wilderness had come to an end was part of one of his more extreme jeremiads. Ousted from the presidency of Harvard, openly flouted by Stoddard and the Brattles, humiliated by the witchcraft fiasco, and denied the apocalyptic vindication he and his son had so confidently predicted for 1700, Increase no doubt derived a certain bitter satisfaction from telling a heedless generation that New England was going to the devil. Without question, the incipient chaos of the 1690's had terminated in virtually total ruin for the Mathers. Yet, given the advantage of a longer perspective, it is possible to see that Mather's pronouncement was literally true. By the beginning of the eighteenth century, the cracks in the foundation of the city upon a hill could no longer be camouflaged. Even to dedicated patriots like the Mathers, it seemed less and less probable that New England was capable of fulfilling the kind of apocalyptic destiny they had initially conceived.

---

[26] Ichabod (Boston, 1702), 80-81.

In his jeremiad, Mather attributed the failure of "the Lords
more peculiar design" to the decay of civil and ecclesiastical
government. Civil and ecclesiastical government in 1702 was not
what it had been under the founding fathers. But this was only
part of the reason New England no longer seemed to have an
apocalyptic destiny. Mather's analysis of the situation, while
accurate, was actually little more than a tautology. Since New
England had been divinely commissioned to provide model
specimens of civil and ecclesiastical government, their decay
necessarily implied failure. Actually, there had been many
forces at work undermining the apocalyptic vision that was the
foundation of the New England Way throughout the seventeenth
century. When these coalesced in the century of enlightenment,
it became painfully clear, even to a Mather, that the New
England Way was somehow at odds with the new century.

Of all the elements in the congeries of opinion, idea, and
feeling that made up the intellectual climate of the new age,
perhaps the one most profoundly at odds with apocalyptic thought
was the growing desire of men to simplify the universe.
Everywhere thoughtful men interested in the "new philosophy"
were observing the world with critical eyes and formulating
their observations in terms of simple yet comprehensive laws.
There was a tremendous impulse to clear away the trimmings of
perception, to get at the structure of reality. The
philosophical system of Descartes, the sensational philosophy of
Locke, the empirical method of Bacon, and the new physics of
Newton were all aimed in one way or another at reducing the
complex and varied world of the senses to its simplest
components. Increasingly men began to think in terms of a
predictable, ordered universe. Such a universe had no place in
it for chosen peoples or special missions. To men who were
interested in discovering an empirical answer to the question of
why things happened as they did, the idea that all events could
best be explained by attributing them to God's providence was
rapidly becoming unsatisfactory. Such an idea postulated the
arbitrary and empirically inexplicable intervention of God in
the affairs of the world. Yet the essence of the conception of
New England's apocalyptic mission was that the colony was a
special historical expression of divine purpose. In the
eighteenth century, it began to seem less and less likely that

God revealed Himself to men in specific historial events--of
which miracles were the most obvious example--and that instead
the truest revelation of the nature of God was imbedded in the
very structure of "reality." The key to true knowledge of
divinity as of everything else lay in man's God-given ability to
apprehend the order inherent in the physical and moral
universe. Mankind had no need of the judgment of
history--whether past or future, limited or universal--in order
to fathom God's purpose in creation.

New Englanders themselves had already done much to lessen
the impact of eschatological judgment in their own hellfire
sermons. As we have seen, hellfire preaching had first been
emphasized in the hopes that it would trigger an outpouring of
the Spirit by bringing home to the individual the horrors of
Judgment Day for impenitent sinners. Ironically, this kind of
preaching was most efectively used by Solomon Stoddard. When he
manipulated it, the Doomsday sermon became an unrivaled
instrument for the conversion of second-generation Puritans.
Spurred by the sign of his fruitful "harvests," the colony's
ministers redoubled their earlier efforts in this direction.
After all, unless they wished to attribute Stoddard's success to
his innovations in church membership, they had to regard the
effusions of the Spirit upon Northampton as the result of his
preaching. There was an appreciable increase in the number of
sermons on the horrors of hell and delights of heaven as the end
of the seventeenth century approached. The number did not
dwindle in the next century. Persuasions from the terror of the
Lord were staple Sunday fare for New England church-goers,
though it is hard to believe the prosaic pronouncements of some
of the ministers had much effect on their congregations'
behavior. Benjamin Wadsworth, for instance, began one such
sermon with the statement that "though in this World, the Godly
often meet with great Adversity, and the Ungodly with great
Prosperity: yet hereafter it will evidently appear, that the
former, viz. the godly, took a wise and safe Course; and the
latter, viz. the Ungodly, took a very foolish and dangerous
one. For however it fares with Persons in this present Life,

154

yet in the Judgment Day, every one shall be dealt with <u>according
to his Works</u>."[27]   Nor did he end on a more inspiring note: "<u>We
should firmly believe the Resurrection of the dead, the coming
of Christ in Glory to Judge the World, and to reward every Man
according to His Works</u>.   These things, the <u>Infallible Word of
God</u> plainly declares to us, and they are the strongest Arguments
& Motives to true Piety; therefore we should most firmly believe
them, and continually realize the truth of them to our own
Souls."[28]

These sermons with their threats of punishment and promises
of reward slowly but surely transformed the Day of Judgment from
the consummation of history into a mere sanction for morality.
Instead of regarding Doomsday as the moment in which "the whole
Context and coherence of it [providence] shall be set together,
and the full History of all the world produced before the
Saints," men began to think of it only as the occasion upon
which the saved would be separated from the damned for all
eternity.   The concomitant of this transformation was a loss of
the sense of the imminence of the Last Day.   From emphasizing
its importance as a sanction for individual morality, the
ministers moved to a consideration of the significance of
death.   For all practical purposes that was the moment when each
individual's fate was decided, and while no man knew with
certainty the hour of the end of the world, every man did know
that he must die one day.   Unless there were strong reasons for
believing that Christ would return before he died--reasons which
the clergy were increasingly unable to supply--the fear of death
would logically take precedence over the fear of Judgment Day.
As Samuel Moody warned the vain youth of New England in 1701,
"nor should the distance of this Great Day make it less awful to
any of us: For there will be a Day of Particular Judgment,
which shall unalterably determine our final and everlasting
Estate, as soon as our Souls are separated from our Bodies,

---

[27]<u>Twelve Single Sermons on Various Subjects Tending to
Promote Godliness</u> (Boston, 1717) 194-5.

[28]<u>Ibid.</u>, 213-214.

Heb 9.27, Which may be the case of the Youngest of us all,
within a very few Days or Hours; . . . And truly, the General
Judgment may be nearer than we imagine. The Lord may come
unlook'd for, and surprise Young Ones in the midst of their
Carnal Mirth and Jollity."[29]

Only a few years later, the clerical spokesman for polite
society in Boston, Benjamin Colman, made it clear that men of
learning and culture were no longer interested in determining
the time of the Last Judgment. In an exposition of the parable
of the ten virgins obviously meant to be compared with Thomas
Shepard's classic, Colman deliberately chose to treat
exclusively of Christ's coming at death rather than His coming
at the Last Day. With a polish unprecedented in New England
sermons, Colman expounded his theme: "Watch therefore: For your
own Judgment can't be far off; and what is it to us if the
General Judgment-Day be many Ages off, since the Day of our
Death is certainly very nigh."[30] When he did speak of the end
of history, he took the occasion to snub Increase and Cotton
Mather. "Some good Men have been too Curious and Positive in
fixing the Periods of Revolutions that are prophecy'd of; and
have been rebuk'd for their bold Conjectures, by living to see
themselves confuted."[31] The Mathers had cried wolf once too
often for their compatriots to take them seriously any longer.

It was not long before the clergy began justifying the Day
of Judgment more from "rational" grounds than from biblical
prophecies. Henry Flynt preaching in 1714 on the doctrine of
the Last Judgment told his listeners that the grounds for
believing in Judgement Day are partly from natural light and
reason and partly from Scripture revelation. Reason, he said,

---

[29]The Vain Youth Summoned to Appear at Christ's Bar (3rd
ed.; New London, Conn., 1760), 8-9.

[30]Benjamin Colman, Practical Discourses upon the Parable
of the Ten Virgins (London, 1707), 421.

[31]Ibid., 419.

teaches that God is good and hates sin. Hence He must reward
virtue and punish vice in order to be consistent with His
nature. This infers a future judgment since "we do not find
that Vertue and Vice are thus equally treated in this World:
. . .The dispensations of Divine Providence are very promiscuous
to the good and bad in the present State."[32] Just as the
nature of God and His providence infer a future judgment, so
does the nature of man. For man is a reasonable creature,
capable of moral actions, with free powers of choosing good and
refusing evil. "It can never be supposed that God has thus
endowed Man for Nothing, and that He will never hereafter take
any Notice of His Improvement of so much Time, and such rich
Endowments conferred upon him." This would be to no purpose and
cannot be reconciled with the wisdom of the Creator and Governor
of things. Besides, "why does Natural Conscience in Men Accuse
and Excuse them in their Actions, If there were no Judgment of
God, and they were never to be accountable to Him?"[33] The
welcome which New England ministers extended to this fashionable
reason was not without reservations. In the preface Increase
Mather wrote for Flynt's sermons, he acknowledged that a
judgment after death is taught by the light of nature, but he
also commended Flynt for preaching salvation through faith and
not mere morality.

There was a very real danger that salvation would be
transformed into mere morality, but the danger was less and less
recognized by New England ministers as the eighteenth century
progressed. In spite of his father's doubts Cotton Mather with
typical ingenuity even contrived to bring his ever-green
apocalyptic expectations up to date. He was encouraged in this
endeavor by a correspondence with the German pietist, August
Francke, on the ecumenical and eschatological
implications of missionary work. Both men were deeply
interested in converting the heathen and had lent their support
to specific missions--in Mather's case missions to the American
Indians and in Francke's, missions to Africa. When they learned

---

[32]Henry Flynt, The Doctrine of the Last Judgment Asserted
and Explained (Boston, 1714), 4.

[33]Ibid.,5.

of each other's efforts, they hastened to set forth their
respective ideas on the significance of world missions.
According to Cotton, the major impetus to missionary work was
the knowledge that these were the days immediately preceding the
Lord's coming and that therefore the number of the elect had to
be completed. In this situation he felt the emphasis of the
missionary's teaching should be on the true essence of
Christianity--not upon denominational distinctions. The primary
aim of the missionary was not to perpetuate divisions, but to
endeavor to bring about God's universal Kingdom. In this work
he would be guided by the Holy Spirit, for Mather--true to his
New England heritage--still believed that the propagation of the
Kingdom would be brought about by an effusion of the Spirit. "I
do not know whether the time will be soon at hand which is
appointed by God for the pouring out of the Holy Spirit and
whether the Kingdom of God will be revealed soon. I believe,
however, that it is at hand."[34]

Mather did not confine his ideas on the subject to private
correspondence. In 1717 he published a work entitled _Malachi_,
which was intended to show that the "_Recovery_ of the Church, and
of Mankind, unto Desirable Circumstances, must be by a lively
Propagation of _Real_ and _Vital_ PIETY in the World."[35] By
desirable circumstances he meant the millennium. He expected
piety to bring it on by setting forth religion in terms which
could be understood by men all over the world. Defining piety
in three fundamental maxims--"the very Life and Soul of the
CHRISTIAN RELIGION"--Mather optimistically asserted that "the
Morality of our _Everlasting_ MAXIMS, is discovered, inculcated,
required, even by the _Light of Nature_ it selfe."[36] Since this
was so, all that was required to initiate the millennium was
that men be induced to follow the promptings of the light of
nature. Mather even had an idea on how to bring this about:

---

[34]From a letter written in 1717, quoted in Ernst Benz,
"The Pietist and Puritan Sources of Early Protestant World
Missions," _Church History_, XX (June, 1951), 50.

[35]Cotton Mather, _Malachi_ (Boston, 1717), 4.

[36]_Ibid._, 37.

It may be proposed, That there should be formed SOCIETIES of Good Men, who can own some such Instrument of PIETY, and make it their most inviolated Law, to bear with <u>Differences</u> in one another upon the <u>Lower</u> and <u>Lesser</u> Points of <u>Religion</u>, and still at their Meetings have their <u>Prayers</u> for the growth of the People, who being Established on the Grand MAXIMS of Christianity are to become a <u>Great Mountain and fill the whole Earth</u>, accompanied with Projections of the most <u>unexceptionable Methods</u> to accomplish it.

GOD alone knows; what <u>wonders</u> He would please to do, both <u>for</u>, and <u>by</u>, Good Men <u>Associating</u> for such Glorious Purposes.[37]

Clearly by 1717 Mather had departed radically from the apocalyptic vision set forth by his grandfather, John Cotton. His apocalyptic expectations no longer had a place for the conception of a regenerate church in a model state to serve as "a <u>Specimen</u> of what shall be over all the Earth in Glorious Times which are Expected." The apocalyptic vision had at last become totally divorced from the pursuit of ecclesiastical purity which had first brought the Puritans to America. With the advent of the eighteenth century, New England eschatology was so rationalized and individualized that it became difficult to relate the end of the world to the community as such. Of the two eschatological boundaries dividing present and future existence--one for the individual and the other for all Creation--death was gradually becoming the more important. By the time the eighteenth century was well under way, death's imminence was far more real and meaningful to New Englanders than the possibility that Christ might return at any moment to judge the quick and the dead. Slowly but surely the focus of New England's eschatological concern had moved from the historically conditioned community to the individual and his eternal problem of salvation. Inevitably this shift marked the end of the New England Way.

---

[37]<u>Ibid.</u>, 92-3.

BIBLIOGRAPHY

Very little work on Puritan eschatology has been done,
although there are indications of a growing interest in this
topic. (See, for instance, John Wilson's article on John Canne
in Church History.) Karl Loewith's Meaning in History was
particularly valuable in helping me conceptualize this study.
Edmund Morgan's study of the New England conception of the
regenerate church (Visible Saints: The History of a Puritan
Idea) is essential for a clear understanding of Puritan
eschatology in New England, as is William Haller's work on John
Foxe's Book of Martyrs. T. F. Torrance's book on the
eschatology of Calvin, Luther, and Bucer (Kingdom and Church: A
Study in the Theology of the Reformation) is illuminating and
helped me understand the relationship between the Puritan
conception of the church and their conception of history. LeRoy
E. Froom's The Prophetic Faith of Our Fathers: The Historical
Development of Prophetic Interpretation is a useful source of
bibliographical references for works dealing with the end of the
world. His commentary on these works, however, is distorted by
his preoccupation with pre-millennialism. James P. Martin's The
Last Judgment in Protestant Theology from Orthodoxy to Ritschl
contains a section on Puritan eschatology, though in fact he
discusses only Solomon Stoddard, Richard Baxter, and Jonathan
Edwards. His treatment of other Protestant theologians,
however, is valuable. Finally, like every student of New
England Puritanism, I am deeply indebted to Perry Miller's
work--perhaps more so than others, since his volumes on the New
England mind are responsible for originally arousing my interest
in the Puritans.

Primary Material

Adams, William. The Necessity of the Pouring Out of the Spirit.
    Boston, 1679.

Allin, John and Shepard, Thomas. "The Preface . . . before
    their Defence of the Answer Made unto the Nine Questions."
    In Massachusetts, or the First Planters of New-England, the
    End and Manner of their Coming Thither and Abode There.
    28-40, Boston, 1696.

Alsted, Johannes H. The Beloved City or the Saints Reign on Earth a Thousand Yeares. Translated by William Burton. London, 1643.

Anonymous. "New England's First Fruits" In Samuel E. Morison, The Founding of Harvard College, 419-447. Cambridge, Mass., 1935.

Bale, John. Select Works of John Bale. Edited by Henry Christmas. Parker Society Publications, I. Cambridge, 1849.

Beza, Theodore. A Briefe and Pithie Summe of the Christian Faith. Translated by R. F. London, 1566.

Brightman, Thomas. The Revelation of S. Iohn Illustrated with an Analysis and Scholions. 3rd edition. Leyden, 1616.

Broughton, Hugh. A Revelation of the Holy Apocalyps. 1610

Bulkeley, Peter. The Gospel-Covenant or the Covenant of Grace Opened. 2nd edition. London, 1653.

Bradford, William. Of Plymough Plantation: 1620-1647. Edited by Samuel E. Morison. New York, 1952.

Bullinger, Heinrich. One Hundred Sermons on the Apocalypse of Iesu Christ. Translated by John Daws. London, 1573.

Calvin, John. Institutes of the Christian Religion. Translated by Henry Beveridge. 2 vols. Grand Rapids, Michigan, 1953.

Colman, Benjamin. Practical Discourses upon the Parable of the
     Ten Virgins. London, 1707.

Cotton, John. The Churches Resurrection. London, 1642.

------------. An Exposition upon the Thirteenth Chapter of the
     Revelation. London, 1655.

------------. Gods Promise to His Plantation. London, 1630.

------------. The Keyes of the Kingdom of Heaven and Power
     Thereof According to the Word of God. London, 1644.

------------. Of the Holinesse of Church-Members. London,
     1650.

---------------. The Powring Out of the Seven Vials. London,
     1642.

---------------. A Sermon Preached . . . at Salem, 1636.
     Boston, 1713.

Cushman, Robert. A Sermon Preached at Plimouth in New-England.
     London, 1622.

Danforth, John. Judgment Begun at the House of God and the
     Righteous Scarcely Saved. Boston, 1716.

Davenport, John. Another Essay for the Investigation of the
     Truth in Answer to Two Questions. Cambridge, Mass., 1663.

Davenport, John. An Answer of the Elders of the Severall
     Churches in New-England unto Nine Positions Sent over to
     them. London, 1643.

---------------. A Discourse about Civil Government in a New
     Plantation Whose Design is Religion. Cambridge, Mass.,
     1663.

Eliot, John. A Brief Narrative of the Progress of the Gospel
     Amongst the Indians in New-England in the Year 1670.
     London, 1671.

----------. The Christian Commonwealth or the Civil Policy of the Rising Kingdom of Jesus Christ. London, 1659.

----------. Communion of Churches. Cambridge, Mass., 1665.

----------. The Dying Speeches of Several Indians. Cambridge, Mass., 1683

-------------and Mayhew, Thomas, Jr. The Glorious Progress of the Gospel Amongst the Indians in New England. Edited by Edward Winslow. London, 1649.

----------. A Further Accompt of the Progresse of the Gospel Amonst the Indians in New England. London, 1659.

----------. A Late and Further Manifestation of the Progress of the Gospel Amongst the Indians in New-England. London, 1655.

----------and Mayhew, Thomas, Jr. The Light Appearing More and More Towards the Perfect Day. Edited by Henry Whitfield. London, 1651.

-------------and Mayhew, Thomas, Jr. Tears of Repentence. London, 1653.

Flynt Henry. The Doctrine of the Last Judgment Asserted and Explained. Boston, 1714.

Forbes, Patrick. An Learned Commentarie vpon the Revelation of Saint Iohn. 2nd edition. Middelburg, 1614.

Goodwin, Thomas. The Works of Thomas Goodwin. Edited by John C. Miller. 12 vols. Nichol's Series of Standard Divines. Puritan Period. Edinburgh, 1861-66.

Higginson, John and Hubbard, William. A Testimony to the Order of the Gospel in the Churches of New-England. Boston, 1701.

Hooke, William. A Discourse Concerning the Witnesses, Relating to the Time, Place and Manner of their Being Slain. London, 1681.

--------------. Letter to John Davenport, 1664. Copy made by
   G. Lyon Turner, Beinecke Library, Yale University.

--------------. A Short Discourse of the Nature and Extent of
   the Gospel-Day. London, 1673.

Hooker, Samuel. Righteousness Rained from Heaven. Cambridge,
   Mass., 1677.

Hooker, Thomas. The Danger of Desertion. London, 1641.

Johnson, Edward. Wonder-working Providence of Sions Saviour in
   New England. Edited by William F. Poole. Andover, Mass.,
   1867.

Lee, Samuel. The Great Day of Judgement . . . Accompany'd with
   Preparatory Meditations upon the Day of Judgement by Mr.
   Cotton Mather. Boston, 1692.

Mather, Cotton. Eleutheria Or an Idea of the Reformation in
   England. London, 1698.

--------------. India Christiana. Boston, 1721.

--------------. Magnalia Christi Americana. Edited by Thomas
   Robbins. Hartford, 1855.

--------------. Malachi. Botson, 1717.

--------------. A Midnight Cry. Boston, 1692.

--------------. Perswasions from the Terror of the Lord.
   Boston, 1711.

--------------. Things for a Distress'd People to Think Upon.
   Boston, 1696.

--------------. Things to Be Look'd for. Boston, 1691.

Mather, Increase. The Day of Trouble is Near. Boston, 1674.

164

----------------. A Discourse Concerning Faith and Fervency in
Prayer and the Glorious Kingdom of the Lord Jesus Christ on
Earth Now Approaching. Boston, 1710.

----------------. A Dissertation Concerning the Future
Conversion of the Jewish Nation. Boston, 1709.

----------------. A Dissertation Wherein the Strange Doctrine
Lately Published in a Sermon . . . Is Examined and Confuted.
Boston, 1708.

----------------. The Doctrine of Divine Providence Opened and
Applyed. Boston, 1684.

----------------. The Greatest Sinners Exhorted and Encouraged
to Come to Christ. Boston, 1686.

----------------. Ichabod. Boston, 1702.

----------------. The Mystery of Israel's Salvation Explained
and Applyed. London, 1669.

----------------. The Order of the Gospel. Boston, 1700.

Mede, Joseph. The Key of the Revelation Searched and
Demonstrated Out of the Naturall and Proper Characters of
the Visions. Translated by Richard More. London, 1643.

-------------. The Works of the Pious and Profoundly-Learned
Joseph Mede. Edited by John Worthington. London, 1672.

Mitchell, Stewart (ed.). Winthrop Papers. Vol. 11, The
Massachusetts Historical Society, 1931.

Moody, Samuel. The Doleful State of the Damned. Boston, 1710.

-------------. The Vain Youth Summoned to Appear at Christ's
Bar. 3rd edition. New London, Conn., 1760.

Norton, John. The Answer to the Whole Set of Questions of the
Celebrated Mr. William Apollonius, Pastor of the Church of
Middleburg. Translated by Douglas Horton. Cambridge,
Mass., 1958.

------------. The Orthodox Evangelist. London, 1657.

Noyes, Nicholas. New Englands Duty and Interest to Be a
    Habitation of Justice and Mountain of Holiness. Boston,
    1698.

Parker, Thomas. The True Copy of a Letter. London, 1644.

Parker, Thomas. The Visions and Prophecies of Daniel Expounded.
    London, 1646.

Perrin, John Paul. Luthers Forerunners or a Cloud of Witnesses
    Deposing for the Protestant Faith. Translated by Samson
    Lennard. London, 1624.

Powicke, F. J. (ed.). Some Unpublished Correspondence of the
    Reverend Richard Baxter and the Reverend John Eliot, the
    Apostle of the American Indians, 1656-1682. Manchester,
    1931.

Sewall, Joseph. The Certainty and Suddenness of Christ's Coming
    to Judgment Improved as a Motive to Diligence in Preparing
    for It. Boston, 1715.

Sewall, Samuel. Phaenomena Quaedam Apocalyptica ad Aspectum
    Novi Orbis Configurata. Boston, 1697.

Shepard, Thomas. The Clear Sun-shine of the Gospel Breaking
    Forth upon the Indians in the New-England. London, 1648.

---------------. Sermons upon the Parable of the Ten Virgins.
    London, 1695.

---------------. A Treatise of Liturgies, Power of the Keyes,
    and of Matter of the Visible Church. London, 1653.

Stoddard, Solomon. An Appeal to the Learned. Boston, 1709.

----------------. The Danger of Speedy Degeneracy Held Forth
    in a Sermon Preached at the Lecture in Boston. Boston,
    1705.

----------------. The Doctrine of Instituted Churches
    Explained and Proved from the Word of God. London, 1700.

----------------. The Efficacy of the Fear of Hell to Restrain Men from Sin. Boston, 1713.

----------------. Falseness of the Hopes of Many Professors. Boston, 1708.

----------------. The Inexcusableness of Neglecting the Worship of God. Boston, 1708.

----------------. The Necessity of Acknowledgement of Offences in Order to Reconciliation. Boston, 1701.

----------------. The Safety of Appearing at the Day of Judgement in the Righteousness of Christ Opened and Applied. Boston, 1687.

----------------. The Tryal of Assurance Set Forth in A Sermon. Boston, 1698.

----------------. The Way for a People to Live Long in the Land that God Hath Given Them. Boston, 1703.

Vincent, Philip. "A True Relation of the Late Battell Fought in New England between the English and the Pequet Salvages." Collections of the Massachusetts Historical Society, 3rd series, V (1836). 29-43.

Wadsworth, Benjamin. Twelve Single Sermons on Various Subjects Tending to Promote Godliness. Boston, 1717.

Webb, John. Practical Discourses on Death, Judgment, Heaven and Hell. Boston 1726.

Whitfield, Henry. Strength Out of Weaknesse. Sabin Reprints. New York, 1865.

Whiting, Samuel. A Discourse of the Last Judgment. Cambridge, Mass., 1664.

Wigglesworth, Micheal. The Day of Doom or a Description of the Great and Last Judgment. London, 1687.

Willard, Samuel. The Checkered State of the Gospel Church. Boston, 1701.

--------------. The Fountain Opened. Boston, 1700.

Wilson, John. The Day-Breaking If Not the Sun-Rising of the Gospell with the Indians in New-England. London, 1647.

Winthrop, John. The History of New England from 1630 to 1644. Edited by James Savage. 2 vols. Boston, 1825.

Secondary Material

Bainton, Roland H. The Reformation of the Sixteenth Century. Boston, 1952.

Benz, Ernst. "The Pietist and Puritan Sources of Early Protestant World Missions," Church History, XX (June, 1951), 28-55.

Bultmann, Rudolf. History and Eschatology. Edinburgh, 1957.

Froom, LeRoy E. The Prophetic Faith of Our Fathers: The Historical Development of the Prophetic Interpretation. 4 vols. Washington, 1946-54.

Haller, William. The Elect Nation: The Meaning and Relevance of Foxe's Book of Martyrs. New York, 1964.

Heimert, Alan. "Puritanism, the Wilderness and the Frontier," New England Quarterly, XXVI (September, 1953), 361-82.

Loewith, Karl. Meaning in History. Chicago, 1958.

Martin, James P. The Last Judgment in Protestant Theology from Orthodoxy to Ritschl. Edinburgh, 1963.

Mew, James. "Thomas Brightman," <u>Dictionary of National Biography</u>, ed. Leslie Stephen and Sidney Lee (1949-50), II, 1247.

Miller, Perry. "The End of the World," <u>William and Mary Quarterly</u>, 3rd series, VIII (April, 1951.) 171-191.

-------------. <u>Errand Into the Wilderness</u>. Cambridge, Mass., 1953.

-------------. <u>The New England Mind: From Colony to Province</u>. Cambridge, Mass., 1953.

-------------. The New England Mind: <u>The Seventeenth Century</u>. Cambridge, Mass., 1954.

Morgan, Edmund S. <u>The Puritan Dilemma: The Story of John Winthrop</u>. Boston, 1958.

----------------. <u>Visible Saints: The History of a Puritan Idea</u>. New York, 1963.

Niebuhr, H. Richard. <u>The Kingdom of God in America</u>. New York, 1937.

Nuttal, G. F. <u>The Holy Spirit in Puritan Faith and Experience</u>. Oxford, 1946.

-------------. <u>Visible Saints: The Congregational Way, 1640-1660</u>. Oxford, 1957.

Pearce, Roy H. "Ruines of Mankind: The Indian and the Puritan Mind," <u>Journal of the History of Ideas</u>, XIII, (April, 1952), 200-217.

Pettit, Norman. "The Image of the Heart in Early Puritanism: the Emergence in England and America of the Concept of Preparation for Grace." Unpublished Ph.D. dissertation, Department of American Studies, Yale University, 1962.

Quistorp, Heinrich. <u>Calvin's Doctrine of Last Things</u>. Translated by Harold Knight. London, 1955.

Spini, Giorgio. "Riforma Italizana e Mediazioni Ginevrine nella Nuova Inghilterra Puritana." In Ginevra e L'Italia. Florence, 1959.

Sprott, George W., "Patrick Forbes," Dictionary of National Biography, ed. Leslie Stephen and Sidney Lee (1949-50), VII, 407-409.

Torrance, T. F. Kingdom and Church: A Study in the Theology of the Reformation. Fair Law, N. J., 1956.

Trinterud, Leonard, J. "The Origins of Puritanism," Church History, XX (March, 1951), 37-57.

Walker, Williston. The Creeds and Platforms of Congregationalism. New York, 1893.

Williams, George H. "The Wilderness and Paradise in the History of the Church," Church History, XXVIII (March, 1959), 3-24.

Wilson, John F. "Another Look at John Canne," Church History, XXXIII (March, 1964), 34-48.

--------------. "A Glimpse of Syons Glory," Church History, XXXI (March, 1962), 66-73.

Ziff, Larser. The Career of John Cotton: Puritanism and the American Experience. Princeton, N. J., 1962.